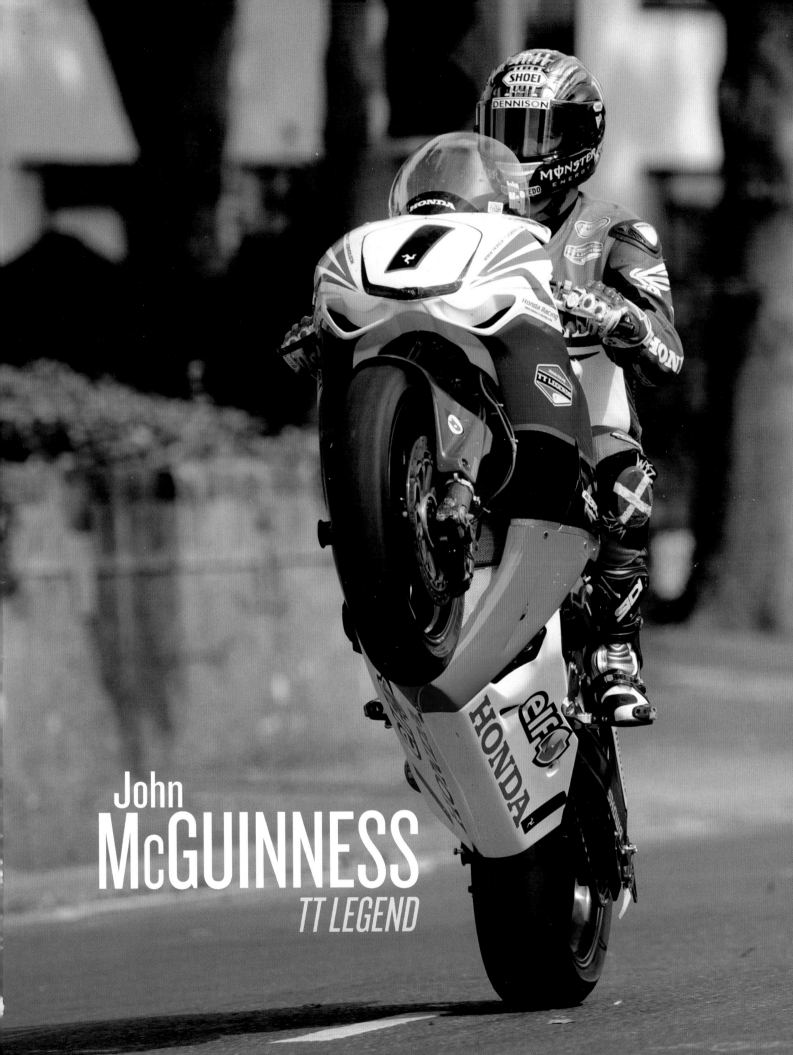

John
McGUINNESS
TT LEGEND

John
McGUINNESS
TT LEGEND

STEPHEN DAVISON

BLACKSTAFF PRESS

He came, he saw, he conquered.
King of the Mountain, John McGuinness,
after the Superbike TT in 2011.

A LOVE AFFAIR WITH THE TT

On the opening night of practice for the 2012 Isle of Man TT John McGuinness was enjoying a rare night off. No sessions were scheduled for the classes that he was competing in. He could have spent the evening commentating for the media or relaxing in the pub but instead John gathered his family and went out on to the course to watch the action at Hillberry.

Throughout the evening he provided a running commentary on the various styles and speeds of the racers as the McGuinness clan leaned over the stone wall to watch them pass just a few inches beneath their noses.

'I can't wait to get out there, to get a lap under me,' he said longingly. 'A fast lap.'

As the evening drew to a close he headed for home with his daughter Maisie Grace perched high on his shoulders. As she blew the seeds off a dandelion head her dad stopped for one last look.

'Isn't that beautiful?' he asked. 'The light beneath the trees, the way the road rises to meet you. That's what the TT is all about, that's why I love it so much.'

Everyone in motorcycle sport is aware of John McGuinness's achievements on the Mountain course. He is the first man to have lapped the incredible 37.74 miles at 130mph and he is currently the holder of the fastest ever lap at 131.578mph. In the last decade he has become 'Mr TT', dominating the event by winning on every type of machine.

By the close of TT 2012 he had added two more wins to bring his total tally of victories to nineteen, securing his position as the second most successful racer in TT history. The only man with more TT success, the late great Joey Dunlop, won 26 TTs in twenty-five years of TT racing. He won his last 3 races at forty-eight years of age. John McGuinness has won 19 races in sixteen years and he celebrated his fortieth birthday in April 2012.

It has been my great privilege to photograph John winning all of those nineteen TT races and to document him establishing his own unique place in the history of the famous Mountain course. There has been great joy in his moments of glory, tempered by days of despair when tragedy has descended upon friends and rivals in this most dangerous of sports.

Behind all of the highs and lows in the shaping of John McGuinness as a true TT legend lies his unyielding passion for the TT and its illustrious tradition, a passion that was etched on his face on that unforgettable evening at Hillberry.

Stephen Davison

BORN TO RACE

'A bit further down here is the first house I lived in in Morecambe,' John McGuinness explains as we meander past rows of Edwardian mansions in the Lancashire town. 'This is the posh end of town,' he says, smiling. 'We lived in the working end.'

A few streets later our tour of his home town takes us into a weed-strewn lane lined with narrow terraces. 'And this is where I rode my first motorbike.'

The 'Morecambe Missile', as the TT legend has become known, is proud of his roots. He has never lived anywhere else since his arrival in the seaside town on 16 April 1972. And it was here, on this scruffy back street behind the little house in which he was born on Granville Road, that the man who would become the world's greatest road racer first threw his leg over a splendid little Italjet at the tender age of three.

'I had stabilisers on the sides and my dad showed me how the throttle worked – back to go, forward to stop,' John remembers. 'And he told me about the brakes. But I just wanted to get going and I set off with the throttle wound open. Dad was running after me screaming and shouting at me to pull the brake, to stop – he thought I was going to go straight into the wall at the back of our house but I just got the bike stopped in time!'

Although his late-braking tactics were the first sign of his daredevilry with an engine beneath him, John had already been living on the edge in his tiny pedal sidecar outfit on these same cobbled back lanes. The earliest photographs in the family album show him proudly perched on a bright yellow three-wheeler accompanied by a huge Alsatian dog called Sam. 'When I would

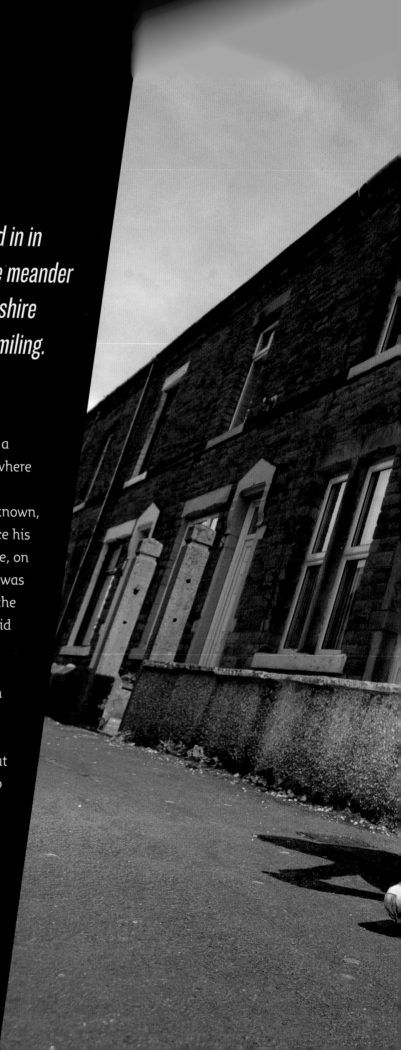

John outside the house where
born on Granville Road in Mor

John – not yet a year old – with his racing father John Senior at a scrambling meeting in 1974.

John with his little yellow sidecar – and Sam the Alsatian who used to steer him back home when he had strayed too far!

disappear down to the end of the road Sam would run along beside me,' John laughs. 'And then he would turn me round with his head and push me back up towards home! On my first day at Sandylands Primary School Sam sat outside the school gates all day waiting for me to come out.'

With all this errant activity going on it wasn't long before the three-year-old had his first brush with the law. 'I had set off on the sidecar along the road and had wandered a few streets away from home. A police car pulled up and asked me where I was going,' John says, smiling. 'I didn't realise that I wasn't allowed on the road on my buggy and they brought me back home.'

Word of the tiny tot's biking prowess quickly spread far and wide. The *Daily Mirror* and a television crew appeared on his doorstep to capture images of the four-year-old jumping a row of toy buses, Evel Knievel style, in his backyard.

The defining motorcycling family influence came from John's father. Racing motorbikes were a permanent feature of the McGuinness household as John Senior raced motocross, grasstrack and short circuits as well as running his own motorcycle sales and repairs business. If he wasn't around the workshop during the week, John was at the races with his dad at weekends and some of these racing forays included trips to the Isle of Man.

'My dad did Jurby road races on the Island in the early eighties and I would go with him and watch. We would take in some of the TT practice and, when I had to go back to school, I would be kicking and screaming on the ferry because I didn't want to go home.'

John's desire to soak up the TT atmosphere eventually led the youngster to stow away on the ferry from Heysham on his BMX bike. 'I'd wait and pedal alongside a van on the blind side and sneak on to the ferry past security,' he smiles.

Proving that a little Evel goes a long way

KNEE HIGH TO A KNIEVEL

The best FUN pictures are in the Mirror

The real Knievel

BRITAIN'S answer ~~~ ~~~
man Evel K~ ~~~
a spectacula~ ~~~
Tiny J~ ~~~

At four years of age daredevil John was making headlines in the *Daily Mirror* and on television stations with his antics on a motorbike. 'Evel Knievel was my hero – he was jumping buses at Wembley and I wanted to be just like him. I had a little stars and stripes suit like his and I jumped toy buses on my Italjet. I even wrote to *Jim'll Fix It* to see if I could get to meet Evel but he never wrote back!'

Such escapades provided the young McGuinness with some unique glimpses of his hero, Joey Dunlop. 'In 1986 I remember seeing Joey riding down the street in Douglas on his works V4 full factory Rothmans Honda. He pulled up on to the pavement, leant the bike against the wall and went into a shop to get fags – he didn't even switch it off! It was the most amazing thing I'd ever seen.'

Soon afterwards John enjoyed a remarkably prophetic encounter with the great man. 'We had heard that Joey was garaging at the bottom of Bray Hill,' John recalls. 'I went to the shop and bought a picture and me and my brother headed down to his garage to get it signed. Joey was spannering away at his bikes and after he autographed it I told him that I would stand on the TT podium with him one day. I was only fourteen. He just looked at me – Joey didn't say much – but in 1997, eleven years later, I did stand beside him up there. And I reminded him then that I had told him I would, but he didn't remember!'

The precocious youngster still had to serve his racing apprenticeship before that date with destiny would

His first diva strop? John refuses to look at the camera as he sulks outside his father's motorcycle shop.

Before there were motorbikes there was a BMX in the McGuinness garage and it was on this trusty steed that John made his first forays to the Isle of Man.

arrive but the die was cast and even though he decided to train as a brickie, his teenage years revolved more and more around motorbikes.

Like so many other sixteen-year-olds in the seventies and eighties John cut his biking teeth on the popular mopeds. A burgundy red AP50 Suzuki was the weapon of choice for the young McGuinness as he blasted around the local laneways imitating his TT heroes, brushing his shoulder off the walls like Steve Hislop and Joey Dunlop. Sometimes the similarity was too close for comfort.

'We had a lot of our own little racing circuits on the roads around here,' John says of those daredevil days as we drive out of Morecambe towards the picturesque village of Heysham. 'A good summer night down here and you're laughing. Me and my mates would chase each other all around these lanes but I had a big near miss down this road one night. My bike had a crap headlamp and I couldn't see where I was going properly – I peeled in too early and clipped this bit of the wall that sits out on the inside of the bend. I took all the skin off my shoulder and I just missed being fired into the wall on the exit. It was a wee fright all right!'

Inevitably John had his first bike crash off the Suzuki. 'The very first one wasn't much – I just tucked the front but I never let go of the bars,'

'A good summer night down here and you're laughing. Me and my mates would chase each other all around these lanes.'

The teenage tearaway on the byways of Morecambe. A seventeen-year-old McGuinness displays some early Ago's Leap style on his TZR 125cc Yamaha. Keeping a watchful eye from the grass verge is his childhood sweetheart Becky, who is now his wife.

In action at Elvington on the KR-1S Kawasaki wearing the orange novice's jacket. This was one of John's first races.

Proudly displaying some of the haul of silverware from his first season of racing.

The Shell Oils scholar suited and booted in 1992.

he justifies in the usual racer's style. 'But I had a bigger one later on at our "Ballaugh Bridge". It was a bridge at Bolton-le-Sands, a couple of miles away, and there was a pub beside the bridge where everyone would sit outside on a summer evening so you had to put on a good show. One night I got a really big jump but a guy pulled out of the pub car park just as I came over and I couldn't avoid him. His driver's window was open and I went straight through it and hit him on the head! It's funny, I bumped into the guy a couple of years ago in the same pub and he remembered me doing it – I said I was sorry!'

Like every moped-restricted teen, John couldn't wait to graduate to something more powerful when he turned seventeen and he scraped together enough cash from gathering mussels on Morecambe Sands to purchase a pristine red and white Yamaha TZR125. The increase in power boosted his bravado and as the speeds got higher so too did the jumps and wheelies, activities that brought him to the notice of the local constabulary.

'I had given up the bike shop and was working on the oil and gas rigs at the time,' his father John Senior recalls. 'Every time I came home on leave I heard stories about John's antics and local coppers warned me that he was getting a bit too wild. So that's when we decided to go racing with a Kawasaki KR-1S.'

when you're a kid you think that you can do anything, don't you?' John reflects. 'I thought that I was dead fast around here but my dad put it up to me – "Okay, so you think you're good, then we'll go racing and see if you are."'

John's first ever race was a club race at Aintree at the end of 1990. 'I was beaten by two girls that day,' he says, smiling ruefully. But he wasn't deterred. 'In 1991 we did a full season of club races. We didn't really have a plan, it was just a case of doing some races and seeing how we got on, see if I could do any good really.

I did the first round of the British Clubman's series at Mallory Park in the pouring rain in 1991 and I won, so we did the rest of the series and by the end of the year I had won the championship.'

It was a promising start and the following year John was awarded the Shell scholarship,

a bursary that was aimed at supporting young ri as they learnt their craft. Over the next three yea Morecambe man doggedly pursued that path, rc week in, week out in the British 250cc champion on the short circuits.

In 1994 he made his road racing debut at the West 200 but it was to be two more years before McGuinness would cross the Irish Sea to line up Glencrutchery Road for the first time.

'I went to the TT in 1990 on my KR1-S Kawasaki with Be we stayed in Port Erin. I was riding past the paddock or and I saw Joey Dunlop's van parked up. I pulled up to g to take a picture of me and my bike beside it.' It might j quick snapshot of an eighteen-year-old kid on his moto it not for the incredible racing history that links this ph with the Isle of Man TT races. Within seven years John were sharing TT podiums and within ten years the pair team-mates in the Vimto Honda squad as they progres towards becoming the two greatest TT racers of all tim

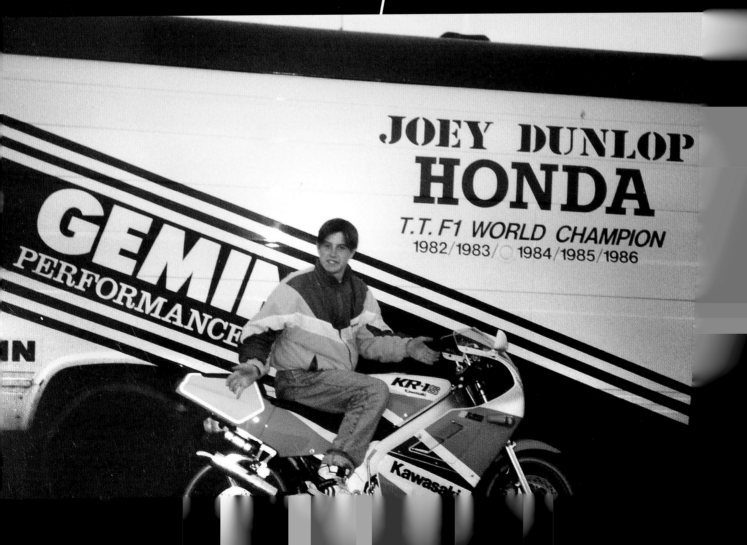

1996 DEBUT

Having served his time on the British short circuit scene and cut his teeth on the Irish roads it was only a matter of time before John would make his TT debut. But even as a rookie he felt that there was no point in going to the Island unless he had the machinery to allow him to make the most of the opportunity. By 1996 he felt he had the experience and the bike that he needed to begin but there were troubles ahead that he could not prepare for.

'I thought doing the TT was the coolest thing in the world. I always wanted to be a TT racer so I suppose it was meant to be but I didn't really know how I was going to do it, how I was going to approach it.

'I thought about doing the Manx and I had my own TZ250 Yamaha but we never had a pot to piss in and I couldn't afford to buy any new bits for the bike. I've always believed with the TT that if you can't do it properly it isn't worth doing. And I wanted to grow up a bit first as well, to get some experience and understand what bikes and racing are about.

'I went to the North West 200 in 1994 and again in 1995 and I was just about scraping into the top ten. But when I went back in 1996 on the new Paul Bird Motorsport Honda RS250 with a few quid to spend on parts I was bang in front of the race with Phillip McCallen, Joey Dunlop, Woolsey Coulter and Robert Dunlop. All these absolute greats and I'm dicing for the lead with them.

'I sat down with Birdy afterwards to talk about the TT and it was a bit of a joke really – I said "Will we do it?" And he said, "If you want to." So I rang up and got a late entry and we just rocked up, starting at number 71 in practice.

'I got £350 from the Mike Hailwood Foundation and £600 travel and start money from the organisers. I thought, if I eat beans on toast for two weeks I'll get through this. One bike, one class, dip my toe in and see if I like it – that was the game.

'On my first ever lap of the course I set off on Monday morning at 5.15 a.m. It was windy, it was cold, it was sunny, it was wet, it was dry and it was damp – four

With starter Andy Fearn's hand on his shoulder, John prepares to begin his first ever TT race, the 1996 Lightweight 250cc event. Riding Paul Bird's RS 250cc Honda John finished 15th and was the best newcomer in the class. 'Look at the front tyre, the boys wheeled it through the mud taking it to the grid. I was mad about that.'

seasons in one lap. And foggy as well! All the things I'd ever been warned about.

'I was behind Mick Lofthouse and Lee Pullan on that first lap. I thought I could maybe stay behind Mick and learn my way round because he was on a 125 but I couldn't stay with him. As I finished the lap I was laughing, thinking that it was horrible. But I was ready for it, I understood what it was going to be like. I had been around the TT and knew some of what to expect. It was still a baptism of fire though.

'Mick Lofthouse was killed in Friday morning practice and Rob Holden was killed on the same lap. I'd raced with Mick for a few years and I was sharing a room with him at the TT. I'd been sleeping in my van and Mick had mentioned it to his landlady at the Monaville Hotel and she told him to bring me in.

'After I heard about Mick, I thought about going home and then I tried to blank it out of my mind. You go through the whole thing in your head about him

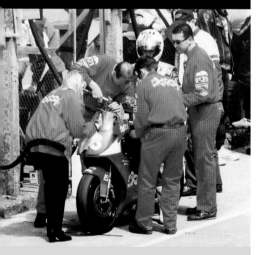

ohn with his sponsor Paul Bird on the Glencrutchery Road before the start of his first T practice session in 1996.
Picture by John Watterson

My first pit stop was pretty cool and calm. The missus is cleaning the screen.'

dying doing something he loved and all the rest but it doesn't help. But going home was never going to achieve anything either, it was never going to bring Mick back. I just said I'd do the race and see how I got on, see how I felt.

'It was a miserable, miserable week of practice, pissing down all the time, cold, with lots of practice sessions called off. I did about 109–110mph in practice and I asked for a start number change and I got shifted up from 71 to 18.

'The race was run on a nice dry day and Joey Dunlop won it. I caught one or two people but it was a pretty uneventful sort of race, always dead safe. That was my approach, I was never going to ride above my station, just bring the bike home. I remember making the team put big jets in the bike to make sure it got round. I finished 15th, did 111.49mph, and was the first newcomer in class. I got a bronze replica.

'My missus, Becky, was in the pits watching out for me and there was no pressure on me. I basically rode round to get a finish.'

Almost home. John comes down to Creg-Ny-Baa from Kate's Cottage on his way to finishing his first TT race on the Paul Bird RS 250cc Honda.

Picture by Terry Howe

HISTORY RECREATED

Anyone who has ever engaged in conversation with John McGuinness about the TT will be able to vouch for his deep interest in and encyclopaedic knowledge of TT history. He can quote you race and lap records from yesteryear or recount tales of Manx racing folklore from the beginning of time. It is no surprise then that he also appreciates his own part in that tradition. Over the years he has amassed an impressive collection of memorabilia from his time of racing on the Island and nothing demonstrates this more clearly than his recreation of his first TT machine, a 1996 RS 250cc Honda.

Since the original bike that John raced in '96 was destroyed in a crash at a 1998 practice at Ballagarey that cost Mike Casey his life so he purchased a similar machine and set about restoring it with the help of close friend Stuart Bland.

'It is identical to how mine was when I went to the TT that year. I learnt my trade on that Honda. It was a real racing bike that taught you about the connection between the throttle and the rear tyre. You had to have a feel for what those needles in the carburettors were doing and that's something that I don't think young lads get nowadays with production-based four-strokes.'

And, as if to prove that that debut year wasn't so far back in time after all, he manages to squeeze back into the original leathers that he wore in 1996 as well. Just!

1997 FIRST PODIUM

It may have seemed like a fairytale to leave the Island as the best newcomer in his debut race in 1996 but in 1997 John went one better and fulfilled a childhood prediction. He was also to make an inauspicious four-stroke racing debut that offered no glimmer at all of the great things that were to come.

'I knew that I would come back to the TT.

'I was still with Birdy and we switched manufacturer to Aprilia for '97. Again we didn't really have a massive plan. We were always pretty flexible about what we did – nowadays people have budgets and settle on what they're going to do for the season. I was doing the 250cc British championship and I rode at Daytona and the North West, where I got a second. I had a 125 for the North West and decided to ride it at the TT as well to give me extra practice and more laps.

'I also rode a 600 Honda at the TT in '97 which wounded me to be honest. I had a blow-up on it in practice and we couldn't get it to handle – it weaved all over the road and it scared me to death for the whole race. It really put me off four-strokes and 600s and I didn't ride a 600 again until 2002.

'The 600 also got me the worst result in all of my TT racing career. I didn't even get a replica and was beaten by Sandra Barnett. I felt really sorry for the owner of the bike – he was a lovely bloke, but I just struggled with it.

'But 1997 was a very significant year because I got my first TT podium, sharing it with Joey and Ian Lougher.

'I just rode round and did my own thing in practice. The 125 seized a few times and Birdy lent me his mobile phone and told me to ring if it seized again. In 1997 not many people had mobile phones and Paul had a fancy one. I put it in my leathers but it fell out and was smashed to bits somewhere on the course!

'In the race the little bike broke a battery terminal at Glentramman. We had a spare battery taped onto the airbox so I borrowed a penny from a marshal and replaced it at the side of the road to get the bike going again. I lost a couple of minutes but it flew after that and I finished twelfth.

'Unlike the 125, my 250 never missed a beat – it was brilliant. I've always said that my Aprilia was so fast that if it had had the right jockey on it, it could have done a 120mph lap. I was blowing people into the weeds on the straights.

'When I was fourteen I asked Joey to autograph a picture for me and I told him that some day I would stand beside him when he won a TT. This was that moment, eleven years later.'

John gets a bit crossed up over Ballacrye in the 250cc race. 'I'm up looking over the top of the screen, you can tell I'm not quite sure how the bike's going to react – a bit cautious really. Ballacrye was a lot steeper then, it's flattened out a bit now. But 116.83mph on my second year wasn't hanging about. That little 250 Aprilia was a lovely wee thing to ride.'

'I had start number 26 on the 250 – I went from start number 18 in my first TT, finished 15th and got number 26 the next year. It didn't make any sense.

'I finished third and did the fastest lap of the race, 116.83mph on my last lap, coming in just two seconds behind Lougher. I just kept going faster and faster as the race went along.

'But I was lucky because the third-placed man Gary Dynes broke down. I didn't think I had a chance of winning, I didn't even dream of being on the podium. You know 250cc racing then was really competitive and I was a bit lucky – there were six or seven people who could have won. I just kept my head down and kept out of trouble. I never had any pit boards so I had to wait and see where I ended up. That third was a massive bonus, the icing on the cake.'

John in the winners' enclosure with Joey Dunlop and Ian Lougher after the 1997 250cc race. 'The first time you get on the podium is pretty special. It was all the things I'd ever dreamed of as a kid, to be stood up there with the greats. That's why I've got that big Cheshire cat grin!'

Jumping Ballaugh Bridge on the Clucas 600cc Honda. 'It was a brand new bike with a lovely paint job but I just couldn't ride it, I was rubbish on it. Shocking. It was my worst ever TT race.'

1998 THE HEAVENS OPEN

The fickle nature of TT racing was to become apparent in 1998 after John's sparkling success in previous years. John struggled with machine problems and the unpredictable Manx weather in a race run in conditions that were so appalling it deterred him from racing on wet roads forever.

'1998 was Honda's fiftieth anniversary and there was a lot of expectation of the riders. Honda had everybody that year – Simmo [Ian Simpson], Michael Rutter, Jim Moodie, Phillip McCallen and Joey, the whole job tied up and I was back on Hondas. That was the first year of the Vimto Hondas under Paul Bird Motorsport. So I'd say I was hopeful going in.

'I had an awning full of good tackle. I had a 500cc V twin Honda for that year, a TSR framed 250 Honda and Darren Barton's British championship 125 which was a cramped up little thing. The 500 was weird because the rules didn't allow you to ride it in the Formula One race, just the Senior. I had to sit out the F1 race and I watched at Ballacrye – Simmo won it on the RC45.

'It was an awful year for weather. In the 250cc race it just poured down but it had started off damp and we had intermediates on. [Former world champion and TT winner] Brian Reid was helping us a bit and he said, "Whatever you do don't stop to change the tyres. If the mist comes in or they shorten the race you will lose it." Lots of others did stop but I was lying second for most of the race. Joey cleared off and Bob Jackson did a storming last lap and passed me and I finished third in the end.

'It was the worst race I have ever had at the TT. There was lots of standing water everywhere and I was on intermediate tyres. I was young though and I didn't really know any better but I had a couple of big moments on

John splashes through Braddan Bridge on the Vimto 250cc Honda in the Lightweight race. 'It was an awful race, really cold as well as wet. I remember going over the Mountain and thinking the bike was going to seize. The race had been cut at the start to three laps but when I got to Parliament Square, there was a big board saying "Two Lap Race" and I thought, thank God for that!' There were no spectators, nobody was interested and there was nobody at the grandstand either. I was shivering like a shitting dog on the podium.'

Picture by Phil Masters

'With doing the fastest lap of the race in 1997 I was definitely thinking ahead and felt that I was in a strong position to run at the front for the next year. I never really thought that I was an out and out winner though.'

Practice was much drier than race day as John skims the railings at Ginger Hall on the 250cc Vimto Honda.

the Mountain, feet off the peg jobs. From that day on I was never really a lover of wet racing at the TT – that race scarred me forever.

'The 125 broke down in the race but I had my first big bike ride in the Senior on the 500 V twin. I was heading for the first 120mph lap on the last lap, looking like

I would get fifth or sixth just riding round, enjoying myself, picking up speed. I remember coming into the pits for my last fuel stop and they were timing the fuel in and all that stuff. They asked me if I wanted a drink and I said no, fill the tank. They asked me again and I told them no again, just fill the tank. They shut the cap

John looks a little worried in
the pits during 1998 practice.

Exiting Rhencullen on the 500cc Vimto Honda in the Senior TT.
'I was suicidal when it ran out of petrol at the 33rd on the last lap.'

Wheelieing
through the rain
on the approach
to Ramsey in the
250cc race.

and I remember thinking I hope I've enough petrol to
get to the finish.

'The bike was singing along, I was heading for
a 120mph lap, top six finish, a bit of prize money,
everything was good until I got to the 33rd Milestone
and it ran out of fuel. I was suicidal.

'There was nobody around. I just sat on the bank
and then I heard Michael Rutter coming on the RC45,
droning across the Mountain. I thought, "My God that
is so fast." It was really impressive.

'My lip was out a bit afterwards but I liked the bigger
bike and it was another part of serving my trade.'

John gets tucked in on the TSR framed 250cc Vimto Honda at Ballaspur on the way to his maiden TT victory in 1999. 'It was time to win. That bike was amazing. I qualified on the front row of every British championship race that year and I finished on the podium of every race too. I had such a fantastic year, riding on a crest really.'

Harnessing the momentum of a successful early season in America and on the British championship scene, John was to make his boyhood dream come true by winning his first TT race in 1999. The essentials of the formula that would provide much of the twenty-seven-year-old's later success can be found in the strategy he used to claim that maiden victory.

'I never, ever predict anything but I was quietly confident that I could give the boys a run that year in the 250cc race at the TT. I was leading the British 250cc championship at the time, had been to Daytona in March and had won the 250cc race there so I was hitting the ground running really.

'I absolutely adored my 1999 250cc TSR Honda and to be brutally honest it was by far the fastest bike on the track. It had a factory "A" kit on it, trick parts. I remember going down Bray Hill on the first lap and thinking if I don't win the race on this bike I will never win – I've had three years doing this, I know where I'm going, it is time to win.

'Jim Moodie was giving me a run for my money on the Padgett's bike before he broke down and James Courtney crashed in front of Joey, which ruined his race, so maybe I got a little bit lucky. But then I broke Ian Lougher's longstanding lap record. I was well happy.

'I had concentrated on the start, broken the lap record from a standing start, and then went even faster on the second lap. I had a good pit stop which gave me a forty-five-second lead. I passed Denis McCullough and Owen

John gets a kiss from his girlfriend Becky after the podium celebrations in 1999. 'She has always been with me – we've been together through all the ups and the downs.'

McNally to lead on the road. I just cruised to the finish. It was great weather, a great race to be involved in.

'It was a bit of "Thank God for that, we've won one" afterwards because a lot of effort, a lot of time and money and practice had gone into that first win. It was one that I wanted and it made me hungry for more.

'After 1999 my career changed direction a bit and I shifted on to bigger bikes. I probably should have done it a bit earlier really because that's where the kudos is.

'I didn't have very good races in the Formula One or Senior races in 1999 on the 500 V twin Honda though. I was struggling a bit. I had a big slide at the Verandah

John follows his TT hero Joey Dunlop through Rhencullen on the second lap of the Senior TT in 1999. 'Joey had passed me at the Wagon and Horses and I followed him round which was amazing as I had never really ridden with him on the track before. That was a special experience – I was hanging on to the back of him thinking "That is William Joseph going around the TT and I am right behind him."'

on lap two of the F1 race after the bike bust a seal and leaked oil over the back wheel, so I had to retire. In the Senior I was fifth fastest in practice and things were going well at the start of the race. I came into the pits on lap two and I was lying joint third. I had been getting a tow from Joey after he passed me on the second lap.

'I came round for my pit-stop at the end of the lap and I thought if I can get out behind him again and follow him round maybe I can get a podium here. But then there was a cock-up with the helmet in the pits.

'I went to swap the visor on my helmet and the side pod came off. There was mad panic. I had to change helmets and the mechanic just grabbed another helmet. He jammed it on my head so fast he folded my ears back as well and pulled the strap so tight I could hardly breathe. I just couldn't concentrate like that and I had to stop and fix it. I dropped a load of time and in the end I did my first ever 120mph plus lap but I finished seventh and that wasn't really what I was after.

'But I did get my first ever Honda TT bonus – a black scooter. I've still got it!'

John celebrates with some bubbly after winning his first TT in 1999. 'It's an incredible thing to stand on that podium.'

2000 JOEY'S TEAM-MATE

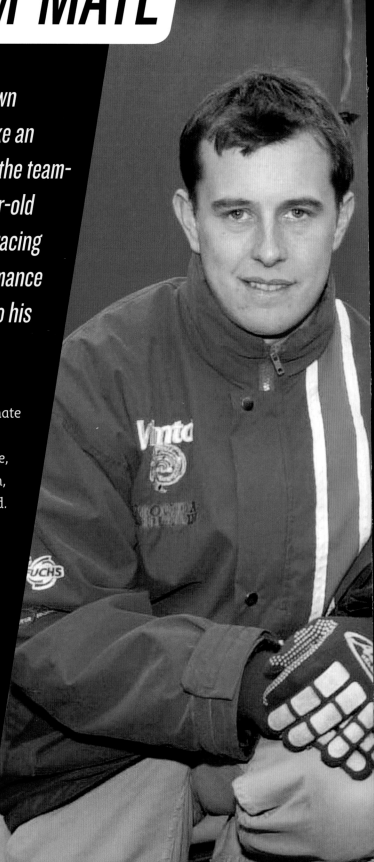

The McGuinness TT tale already read like a Boy's Own storyline after just four short years, but it was to take an almost surreally romantic twist when John became the team-mate of his hero Joey Dunlop as the forty-eight-year-old played out his last act on the world's greatest road racing stage. As Dunlop's incredible treble-winning performance dominated the headlines, few paid much attention to his young protégé's first big bike podium finish.

'2000 was the year I became Joey Dunlop's team-mate – team-mate to my all-time hero.

'I spent a lot of time with the man that year – went to his house, had long conversations with him, shared team briefings with him, travelled together – everything that I had ever dreamed of as a kid.

'And then getting beaten by him again. And again.

'I learnt a lot in 2000 as well when I passed him in practice and cut him up on my 250 at Kerrowmoar. I knew I'd got it wrong and it was the shittest feeling I've ever had in racing.

'I thought I was the kingpin – I was the 250 British champion, I had won the 250 TT the year before, I had the lap record, the best bike, the best of everything. I was too cocky, started being a smartarse. Until I passed him that way and then the penny dropped – you do not do that to the good guys. I knew straight away that he was never going to let me beat him on the 250 after that.

John joined his hero Joey Dunlop in the Vimto Honda squad for the millennium TT. 'I spent the whole time wondering how do you beat this little, forty-eight-year-old fella. And I never worked it out.'

Joey Dunlop won the Formula One TT in 2000 and is flanked on the podium by runner-up Michael Rutter and John in third place. 'The two young pretenders with the King. There are only two days between Michael's birthday and mine and we were nearly twenty years younger than Joey.'

Celebrating his first Superbike TT podium. 'We had a bit of fun up there. Joey couldn't get the top off his champagne and then he dropped the bottle and it spun round in circles on the bottom of the podium. We didn't spray him though, we were too respectful to squirt Joey!'

'I set off ten seconds behind him in the race and I thought I'd catch him and then the job would be done. But I didn't catch him, he just smoked me from a standing start and went on to win it. My bike seized so I got my comeuppance.

'Joey and I were both on the V twin SP1s in the Formula One and Senior races. He had a factory engine – which he absolutely 100 per cent deserved – and I had James Toseland's kit bike. I was really happy with it because I was part of the official Honda factory effort – we had Japanese mechanics and trick new bikes.

'But the SP1 handled like a pig in practice and I hated the thing. I just wanted to get off it and ride my two-stroke 500 instead.

'In the end the team sat down and talked about it. We changed the tyres and found a setting for the race and then we both stuck it on the podium – Joey on the top step and me in third.

'I was happy. It was my first 1000cc four-stroke ride and my first big bike podium, plus the fastest lap I'd ever done at the TT. I was well pleased and it felt like I was moving into the big league!

'The Senior was an interesting race because we put on a thirty-two-litre fuel tank so we would just have one pit stop. But when we set off it was like a half-filled bath because it was so heavy. I lost a lot of time at the start until it used up some fuel and in the end I finished fourth behind David Jefferies, who set the first 125mph lap. Michael Rutter was second and Joey third.

'I also got my second win in 2000 in the Singles race on the Morris brothers' Chrysalis AMDM bike. It was a totally different race as I'd never ridden a big bike like that before but it worked out. It was a great little bike, like riding a slow 250. Some people say it was an easy win but I am proud of it.

John rounds Quarterbridge on the Vimto SP1 Honda in the Formula One race in 2000. 'The road was patchy and damp and I pushed hard, as hard as I could, to get third spot. I went at number 4 trying to catch Joey but that was never going to happen.'

On the Vimto SP1 Honda at Creg-Ny-Baa in the Senior TT with the thirty-two-litre petrol tank that meant he only had to make one pit stop for fuel. 'I could hardly reach the handlebars the tank was so big!'

'I was happy. It was my first 1000cc four-stroke ride and my first big bike podium.'

'There wasn't a lot of pressure on me in 2000 because I wasn't expected to win but I'd had a couple of good results on the big bikes and that helped me get a Honda ride for the short circuits for the rest of the season. It was a step in a new direction and it opened up some doors for me for the future. But you never know what's around the corner in racing. That year I had a TT win, scored my first Superbike TT podium, I was leading the British 250cc championship, won at

Daytona and scored points in the 500cc Grand Prix at Donington. Then I snapped my femur in a crash at Oulton Park and was laid on my back for three months – 2000 season over!

'A month after the 2000 TT Joey was dead, killed in a crash in Estonia. He had always been my hero and to be racing alongside him was so much more than a childhood dream. But almost as soon as it became true, it was over. I was, and still am, devastated.'

John looks to the heavens after winning the Singles race, his second TT victory.

Leaping Ballaugh Bridge in the Singles TT in 2000. 'The Morris brothers had lost both their parents within a week in 1999 and renamed the race bike after them – AMDM – Alison Morris and Dave Morris. Dave had won the Singles TT in 1997, '98 and '99 and to see the boys' faces after I won on their dad's bike in 2000 was really special. I am very proud of that win.'

2002 SACKED!

The foot and mouth epidemic had wiped out most of the 2001 road racing season, including the TT. John arrived on the Isle of Man in 2002 as a full factory rider in Honda colours. The aim was to build on the successes of 2000 on the superbike but even though he got on to the podium twice during the week it wouldn't be enough to keep his ride with the squad for the next season.

'Everything had been going well. I had won the Macau Grand Prix at the end of 2001 but that was almost all the road racing I did that year. I won the Castrol CBR 600 championship in Britain with Honda UK in 2001, and in 2002 I was riding for Honda in the World Supersport championship. Things did seem to be on the up for me. I was making a living out of racing for the first time, but then I started to struggle in the world championship and I got both hurt and sick. I broke my collarbone at a test at Croft early in the season and then I got pneumonia in South Africa. It took me months to get over that and I was really only starting to recover by the time the TT came around.

'I was still involved with Paul Bird because he ran the Superbike and Production bikes for Honda at the TT that year and the World Supersport team looked after the 600s. But my confidence wasn't that great.

'And there was a great big fellow from Yorkshire called David Jefferies who was going to be a big problem as well that year.

'There were two iconic figures on the TT scene in the early years when I was just trying to make my way in the game. Joey Dunlop had been there in 2000 [Dunlop was killed in a race in Estonia in July 2000] and then in '02 it was DJ, but there was no bitterness amongst us. If someone beats you, you have to shake his hand and take it on the chin. Joey had won in 2000 and Dave beat me fair and square in 2002. You just have to accept it.

'By 2002 I was confident I could give David a run for his money but although I had a great bike – and I'm not making excuses – the Honda superbikes were just 954cc and DJ's TAS Suzuki was a 1000cc. There is no

The 'McPint' logo makes its first appearance on the McGuinness leathers at TT 2002.

The factory-Honda rider wheelies out of the Gooseneck in the Formula One race in 2002. 'I never ever put myself under pressure to win and the team didn't either. Throughout my whole racing career it has never been like that, I have just let it happen. I've always done my best but there's nobody else on the bike with you and you're the one that's going to get hurt if you push beyond your limit.'

2002 saw the beginning of a McGuinness family tradition with John bringing his son Ewan to the winners' enclosure after the Formula One and Senior races – even if he did manage to sleep through most of the celebrations! Ewan has never missed one of his father's TTs, and now new addition Maisie Grace, has joined him in the celebrations. 'Ewan isn't really interested in the bike racing but if you have a bit of success he likes to be in there. And if I've had a bad day, a poor result or broken down, kids don't really pay much attention, you're just their dad and that's that. It puts everything into perspective.'

DUKE
FORMULA 1TT
SECOND

2002

substitute for ccs, and the Suzuki was quicker, but in truth he was faster and stronger than me around the Isle of Man at the time, there's no question of that.

'He stuffed it into you in practice and psychologically he would grind you to death. Not in a mean way – DJ was too relaxed and easygoing for that – it was just the way he went about his racing. You would be thinking, if he goes as fast in the race as he went in practice he will take some beating. It got into your head.

'I set off Number 5 in the first Formula One race and finished second, albeit a long way behind DJ. I beat everybody else – Adrian Archibald, Jim Moodie, Ian Lougher, Richard Britton – I was the next best thing.

'I was on my own in the Senior – DJ set off at number 1 and I was at 2. I tried really, really hard to catch him but he just destroyed me. Dave on his day was pretty

unbeatable and, Dave being Dave, he just wanted to completely annihilate us by doing 127.29mph on the last lap when he already had a one-minute lead over second-placed Ian Lougher. He absolutely smashed us to pieces on that last lap and completely raised the bar to another level. I was doing 125s, Lougher did 126 and DJ did a 127 and made us all look pretty average.

'I was the official Honda entrant and racing can be harsh. Overall I had a strong TT – I was dicing for the lead in the 600 race before the bike broke down and I had two good podiums on the big bikes – a second and a third weren't bad results. But there were no wins.

'There was an expectation because I had won before and because I was now a factory rider. It wasn't through lack of trying but it just didn't happen and so the deal with Honda finished. I got the sack.'

John gets a big wheelie through Rhencullen on the Honda Fireblade. 'I beat everybody else to finish second in the Formula One race but I was a long way behind DJ.'

John sweeps under the trees at Tower bends on the Production 600 Honda.

As the sun rises on early morning practice John discusses settings with his mechanics before setting off on a lap. He enjoyed the assistance of a fleet of official mechanics and technicians during TT 2002 but as a result of the parting of the ways with Honda at the end of the year that support would disappear.

David Jefferies set the first ever 127mph lap on the final lap of the 2002 Senior race, winning his third hat-trick of TT races in a row. John and DJ's TAS Suzuki team-mate Ian Lougher could do little more than join in the celebrations of his skill. But this happy moment on the Senior podium was to be the final act of the great man's TT career before tragedy struck in 2003.

John shares the the Formula One TT winners' enclosure with two men who would play big and very different parts in his future TT career – David Jefferies who won the race on the TAS Suzuki and Jim Moodie who finished third on the V&M Yamaha.

2003 DJ'S DEATH

There is an old saying that goes 'Things may be bad today – but that doesn't mean that they can't get worse tomorrow.' If there was ever a year in John McGuinness's TT career that this would be true of, it was 2003.

'At the start of the year I had nothing, no ride at all on the short circuits. The Honda deal had finished so I ended up buying my own bike, building my own 600. I gave that a go for a few races but then I quit because I wasn't getting any support and I was just spending my own money.

'I managed to pull together a deal for the roads riding a factory 600 Triumph for Jack Valentine of V&M, a Monstermob Ducati for Paul Bird and a 400 ride with Ricky Leddy Racing.

'I had to pay Birdy five grand to ride the Ducati at the TT so I needed to find sponsorship. I hadn't really been in that position before so I just took it day by day.

'Looking back it wasn't a bad thing that the Honda deal ended really. It was sort of go away and grow up a little bit and then come back another time. I've always thought that in racing anything can happen, doors open, so you just wait and see what comes your way. With what I had for the roads I knew I could make some pennies and keep the wolf away from the door.

'And then we lost DJ.

'Dave and I were good mates and you always get closer to your mates at the TT because you know what can happen. The two of us had been messing about before the start of practice that Thursday. He elbowed me out of the way because he wanted to go before me and I pushed him back but he was the bigger lad and he muscled in again. I always wonder if I had got away first whether it would have been me that crashed.

John looks to the heavens on the sombre podium after the Formula One race as everyone remembers the death of David Jefferies following his crash at Crosby during practice. 'You can see what we are all thinking, all just having a moment. There was no champagne as a sign of respect. It was fitting really that his team-mate Adrian won but I'd have loved to have won and dedicated it to Dave. Every time I pass the spot where he crashed, on every single lap, I ask him to look after me.'

'He had been struggling earlier in the week but on the first lap he set the fastest speed of practice week, 125mph plus from a standing start, so he was back to his old form. Then, on the second lap at Crosby, the accident happened. I was behind DJ on the road and that meant I was the first to see him after he went down. I stopped my bike and ran back to him but I didn't know what to do, didn't know how to react. I had seen crashes before but I hadn't seen anyone lying in the road like that. Gone.

'I expected Dave to get up and sort of laugh it off but he wasn't moving. Other bikes were coming down the road and slowing down but then Jim Moodie came and he got tangled up in all the wires and the debris on the road.

'I just stood there, just staring at Dave and the bits of bike everywhere, in a sort of trance. It looked like a battlezone.

'Then Big H [Paul Hunt, another racer who had stopped] picked me up and carried me off like I was a little kid. He said there's nothing you can do. I couldn't take it in and I suppose I was in shock. I think that being a fireman, Paul had seen things like that before and he knew the way people reacted.

'The ambulance came and we were told to ride our bikes back to the grandstand. I did consider going home but Dave's mum Pauline said we had to keep on riding, we had to race, and that's basically what we did.

'I found the rest of the TT pretty tough going. In the Formula One race I had to change the tyre because there were chunks of rubber coming off it on lap two and then I lost fourth gear. In the end Archie [Adrian Archibald] just cleared off. I'm not taking anything away from him though, he deserved to win.

'Archie won the Senior as well. I was behind him on the road and I tried and tried to catch him because

John wheelies the Triumph past the spectators lining the bank at the Gooseneck in the Junior TT. He finished tenth.

John at Brandywell on the Monstermob Ducati during the opening evening of practice for TT 2003.

John is flanked by third-placed Ryan Farquhar (left) and by runner-up Richard Britton after the 400cc TT. Richard was to lose his life in a a crash at a race in Ballybunion, Co. Kerry, in 2005. 'You just don't think that it's going to happen to you. You know that it can at any second but you just don't want to believe it. Richard and DJ's careers were cut short so quickly and you ask why; why them and not us?'

I really, really wanted to win a big bike race that year but I couldn't get there. I never caught him and ended up second.

'Kiwi Bruce Anstey won the 600 race and I finished tenth! I tried to win it on the first lap but I outbraked myself at Ballacraine and went straight up the slip road. If you give that time away on a 600 you're beat.

'Looking back I can see now that everything stalled a bit in 2002 and 2003. There were maybe a few stones that I had left unturned, things that I hadn't thought through, and I didn't have the belief in myself that was needed to

John gets close to the crowds as he wheelies the Triumph Daytona out of the Gooseneck during the Junior TT.

On his way to victory in the 400cc TT at Creg-Ny-Baa on the RLR Honda. 'I won the 400 race again that year. 400s take low priority and it's a shame really. I've had three or four wins on them and on the Singles but everything gets concentrated on the bigger stuff and the wee bikes get pushed on to the back burner a bit. Ricky Leddy, the bloke who ran the RLR Honda that year, was putting a lot of effort into it, a lot of his own money, and it was nice to get a win for him.'

beat the big boys. Even though I'd done a few TTs I was still a bit green and David's accident shook everyone up.

'As well as that, my set-up for the TT in '03 was a mishmash because I hadn't really tested the Ducatis and I was riding different bikes in every race – a Honda, a Ducati and a Triumph. I had Dunlop tyres on the big bike and Pirellis on the Triumph and 400. You need more consistency and better preparation than that for the TT and you need a bit of luck.

'But I took another win on the 400 and a couple of podiums. I was learning all the time – and I was still in one piece.'

Jumping the Triumph over Ballaugh Bridge in the Junior TT race in 2003.

Jumping the Monstermob Ducati over Ballacrye in the Senior TT. 'It was nice to beat the Honda in the Senior after having been "released" by the team the year before. I suppose some people might see it as callous that we raced on after Dave's death but it's my job, it's my choice, it's what I do, and it's the only thing that I am good at. It may be selfish but I'm not putting anyone else in danger and racing is selfish. It's also a fun thing to do and the world would be a dull place if there weren't people doing things like that. But I suppose if you're a normal guy you just look at me'

2004 THE FIRST SUPERBIKE WIN

2004 was to see John change manufacturer to Yamaha, bringing a spectacular shift in fortune as he scored his first TT treble which included, perhaps more importantly, his first superbike win.

'In 2004 things started to take off for me at the TT even though all I had at the end of 2003 was a verbal agreement with Yamaha that they would supply me with a superbike for the next season, and only for the TT. I got no mechanics, no team, no back-up in the deal, just the bike. I had to buy another R1 for the North West and finished second to Rutter on it, then I sold it straight afterwards to get my money back. My sponsor Graeme Hanna helped out when he stepped in and provided me with 600s for both events.

'When I got to the TT I saw this big Yamaha truck in the paddock and I thought it must be our wagon so I rocked up with my bikes and bits and bobs. But it was only for Jason Griffiths, who was also on Yamahas, and I was told to leave! I thought because we were riding for the same company we were all working together but we weren't, we were just riding the same colour bikes.

'So we set up our own awning and I sorted a couple of mechanics. We weren't a big outfit but working out of our little Wendy house made me even more determined to beat the bigger teams.

'Jim Moodie was by my side that year and he definitely helped me to focus on what I needed to do to win. He was a mentor, if you like, and I knew he had a lot of experience on the Island. There were a lot of little things that he helped me sort out, things like getting my tear offs right and organising my drinks during the practice and race.

'It was all about attention to detail. Instead of me coming in and messing about between practice laps he was pushing me to the front of the queue so that I could get more laps in. He was guiding me on what I should eat, when I should rest, analysing everything and I was so much better prepared with him by my side.

'Yamaha had asked Rob McElnea to build me a new R1 and I blitzed everybody in the Formula One race on it. It was only a four-lap race that year but I banged in a 127mph lap at the start and that set me up for the one I really wanted, a Superbike TT win.

'The 400 race was the last one run at the TT and I wanted to win it. Riding the little bike was so much fun. The big bikes are frightening things, hitting 180–190mph, but on the 400 the world is going past a bit more slowly.

Wheelieing over Ago's Leap at 170mph in the Formula One race on the R1 Yamaha. 'The bike was fantastic, it was the first time that I had ridden a four-cylinder 1000cc superbike and I broke the lap record in practice and in the race. It was the last ever Formula One race before it went to the new Superbike rules. I've won that race seven times now and I haven't been beaten to this day unless I've broken down.'

'I pushed really hard in the Junior 600 race – getting the lap record up to 122.87mph – and I won the race by a good margin to give me my first TT treble.

'I should really have won five or six races that year. I was dicing for the lead in the 1000cc Production race with Bruce Anstey but I lost a bit of time when I ran short of fuel before the pits and he just beat me to the flag. I was in contention for a win in the Production 600 race as well but finished third after the steering damper snapped going through Glentramman. And I suppose I felt I should definitely have won the Senior but I blew it because of a lack of experience. I had a forty-second lead over Adrian Archibald when I came into the pits at the end of the second lap. As I rolled into the stop box I gave the bike a big handful of clutch, then I gave it another big handful on the way out and I burnt out the clutch. It was the most dickheadest thing you could ever imagine doing. It is so basic I still can't believe I actually did it.'

'I threw that race away and it still eats at me. But you're never too old to learn, especially when you learn the hard way.

'At the end of the day, though, I have to be happy with what was achieved. I won three races, broke the 600 lap record, the superbike lap record, the race record and I took my first big bike win.

'And I realised at last that I could win a superbike race. Up until that day, the day when I actually won on a big bike, I had lacked the belief within myself that I could do it.'

Leading Adrian Archibald on the TAS Suzuki at Brandywell during the Senior TT before the clutch burned out. John had started twenty seconds behind Archie and caught him on the road, giving him a huge lead before he broke down on the third lap.

'I won three races, broke the 600 lap record, the superbike lap record, the race record and I took my first big bike win.'

John shows off his haul of silverware after winning his first TT treble in 2004. 'I've a bit of a glow on my face here because I was happy and proud of what I'd done, really. I was thinking I've got three in a week, I've hit the jackpot and I was in amongst names like Hailwood, Joey, Phillip and DJ who had all done TT trebles. It was a bit of a relief to get there after all the hard work learning the track, learning the bikes, learning everything. But that was where I wanted to be – winning TT races. I realised that, with a bit of luck, I could win if I was working with the right people and had the right tools to do the job. So I was a happy little chappy.'

Catching the last of the sunlight at Tower Bends on his
R6 Yamaha during evening practice. John broke the lap
record on his way to winning the Supersport race.

'The noise of the 400 through the villages like Kirkmichael and Ballaugh reminded me of the V4 Honda days. I had missed out on riding those bikes because my career started too late for them. I felt like Joey Dunlop on the RC30 and it was the last ever 400 race at the TT.'

John jumps Ballaugh Bridge on the RLR Honda on his way to victory in the 400cc race.

John exits the fast left-hand corner after the Gooseneck on the R1 Yamaha superbike. 'Now you're really on the Mountain and this is where you can start making up time. You have to concentrate a lot harder, be bang on line because it's so much faster. After this point it becomes much more open, the walls disappear. You're going uphill so when you shut the throttle it acts like a natural brake and you can really attack the corners a lot more.'

2005 FROM ULTIMATE HIGH TO ULTIMATE LOW

The link with Yamaha continued for John in 2005 but there were significant changes in tyre and helmet deals, deals that continue to this day. This TT would also herald the start of a familiar McGuinness double in the Superbike and Senior races that would underpin his status in the motorcycle racing world as a TT specialist. But John was plunged into turmoil by the death of another close friend in racing that once again would force him to question his very future as a TT racer.

'From the outside it probably looked as if everything was the same for me as it had been in 2004. I was still on the shiny red Yamahas but the job had actually changed a bit for 2005. I had a deal to ride for Alastair Flanagan's AIM Yamaha squad in the British Superbike championship and AIM was also supplying everything for the North West 200 and the TT.

'That year was also the start of my relationship with Dunlop tyres. Before 2005 very few people wanted to ride on Dunlops but then I started to work with them and we developed the tyres. Now Dunlop is the rubber to be on and that was all part of what made 2005 feel like a very different year for me.

'In the Superstock race I was fastest in practice on my own R1 but it was the first TT race I have ever pulled out of. I lost the front end of the bike and had a big slide at Crosby where DJ was killed. That spooked me and my race was over.

'I finished second in the first Supersport race to Ian Lougher and then I broke down in the second one when the bike dropped a valve coming on to the Mountain Mile, the identical spot to within a metre to where it dropped a valve in practice.

'But then I won both the Superbike and Senior TTs. The R1 Yamaha was more or less the same as it had been the year before but I had chosen to go at number 10 instead of the number 3 I had used in 2004. Jim Moodie and I had discussed it and

Start line marshal Andy Fearn's arms are thrown into the air as John blasts off on the Superstock R1. 'I really concentrate on the start. I make sure that the tyres are scrubbed in, that they are as hot as they need to be, so that as soon as that flag drops I can attack the circuit, not have to feel my way into it. Nowadays everybody does that at the start but I was doing it under the radar for three or four years before anybody noticed.'

John gets both wheels off the ground and the front wheel twists as he approaches the bottom on his R6 Yamaha.

The suspension bottoms out on impact with the big recess right on the apex of the corner.

And immediately the suspension extends to its full height as John exits the corner and heads towards the 13th Milestone.

'You've everything to lose and nothing to gain here. Every time I go towards Barregarrow I am cringing and when I hit the bottom it's a big "Oh God" moment. And you always thank the Man Above when you get through it too. Its not a fun place to ride because there's a lot of stress on the bike. But that's what makes it really spectacular to watch.'

thought it might be good to have somebody to chase but it wasn't – I just had more people to pass and that slows you down. The races were back to being six laps after having been just four the year before so it felt like I had done the job properly now.

'I rode well, achieved great things – won two Superbike races, won my first Senior TT – but it was all shattered into insignificance when my friend Gus Scott was killed in the Senior. I was up on the podium after the race shaking champagne like I was the bees knees and then when I came down I was told that Gus had been killed in a crash involving a marshal in Kirkmichael. I went from the ultimate high to the ultimate low in a breath.

'It was really hard to accept, even tougher than DJ's death, because it was so avoidable. Maybe there was some guilt involved as well. Gus was really good fun to be with, mega-witty and sarcastic, right up my street

as a mate. He had talked about doing the TT and I had told him to go for it, encouraged him to race it. He had loads and loads of experience in racing but then he was killed in his first TT. Maybe if I had told him not to do it he would still be here now. I will never, ever advise anyone to race the TT again.

'A lot of things changed in 2005. Before then I had been racing in British and world championships, competing for titles, and then I would go to the Isle of Man and ride the TT. I was a track racer who also did the TT, but after '05 my career started to change and I was regarded more as a TT racer who rode the short circuits at a lower level. That perception can be a bit frustrating at times because even today I still race almost every weekend on the tracks and regularly finish in the top six.

'But then I also know that if I go to the TT and get a couple of good wins I will have a job for the next season.'

Having some fun with Ryan Farquhar, Richard Britton and Adrian Archibald as John pulls in for a 'pit stop' on the replica Shuttleworth Snap (as ridden by George Formby in the TT film, *No Limit*) at the TT press launch in April 2005. 'That's the thing with the TT, the camaraderie with the other riders is great because the bottom line is we all know what can happen if it does go wrong. I've never had a cross word with any of them.'

John's eyes are filled with tears of joy and relief as Becky hugs him in the winners' enclosure after winning the Senior TT in 2005. But triumph turned to tragedy at the podium when he was told his closest friend Gus Scott had been killed in a crash at Kirkmichael.

The spectators get a great view of John exiting Signpost corner on his way to the runner-up spot in the first Supersport race on the R6 Yamaha. Much has changed at the TT since this picture was taken and nowadays access to this whole area is prohibited to spectators. 'It should be like this, I like to see this and these look like a lot of happy people to me. But when things go wrong and people get hurt then there are changes. It's the same with the riders and sadly it's only after one of the top guys gets hurt that there is a shift. That's what happened after DJ's crash – the Number One guy had been taken out and then the questions were asked and action taken.'

John breaks the speed limit at Rhencullen
on his way to his first blue riband class win.

John shares a night out with his three great racing friends David Jefferies, Ronnie Smith and Gus Scott in Macau in 2002. David lost his life in a crash during practice for the TT in 2003, Ronnie was killed in a road accident the same year and Gus was killed in the Senior TT in 2005.

Gettng on to the top step of the podium never comes easy in road racing.

'There is so much life in this picture
and now there is only me left.'

HELMET ART

John McGuinness has one of the most recognisable – and unusual – helmet designs in motorcycle racing. When he first appeared with the original design in 1999 TT fans were mystified by the colour scheme and even today many people are unaware of its origin. The design has a special history and although there is no doubt that John is drawn to the unique swirls and waves of the pattern there is more than a hint of superstition in his choice.

'When I was racing at Daytona at the start of 1999 I crashed in practice and wrote off the helmet I was wearing. I was sharing a garage with a pretty eccentric bloke called Jack Silverman. Jack has a big collection of Pueblo and Navajo Indian artworks in a museum he runs in Santa Fe, New Mexico, and his helmet designs are based on this Indian art. He gave me a helmet to replace the one that I smashed and I won the 250cc race at Daytona. The rest of the 1999 season was the most successful that I'd had in racing up to that point – I won the British 250cc championship, the Scarborough Gold Cup and my first TT – so I stuck with the Silverman design and I've used it ever since.'

John wore Arai helmets until 2005 and then switched to the Shoei brand.

Unlike many motorcycle racers, John keeps almost all of the leathers and helmets that he has raced in throughout his career. He also collects the race gear of other riders.

'This is the Arai helmet I wore on the Hondas in 2002. It is very similar to the original Silverman design that I started using in 1999. The chip on the chin came from cracking it on the fairing after jumping Ballaugh Bridge.'

'I wanted a fancy glitter helmet and I had this painted in 1999. Every time I wore it I had a breakdown or something went wrong. I broke down in the Formula One race when I was wearing it in 1999 and then my mechanic jammed it on my head during the Senior TT pit stop in 1999 after the visor broke on my original lid and I ended up with a bad result. The final straw came when I lent it to Woolsey Coulter in a British championship round and he crashed, so after that I retired it!'

This helmet was worn by John when he won the last ever Singles TT in 2000. The scratch is from a short circuit crash.

'This was the third helmet that Jack Silverman sent me and I liked it. I decided to wear it at Oulton Park in 2000 for the first time, went out of the pits, got to Shell Oils hairpin, accelerated out of it, high sided, crashed and broke my leg – it had been on my head for three minutes! That sealed the whole deal about sticking to the original design that Jack had given me. It's weird – I blame the helmet but I know that it really has nothing to do with the helmet. No matter what, I always revert back to that original design though.'

'I had the same design on the Arai in 2003 and 2004 but I don't have the original helmet that I wore when I won my first big bike TT in '04 because I swapped it with Michael Rutter for one of his. I was wearing this particular helmet when I crashed the Hawk Kawasaki at Scarborough during the Gold Cup in September 2004 and wrecked it.'

John kisses the voodoo doll on the back of his helmet before the start of the Superstock TT in 2011. 'I didn't always kiss the doll but I started doing it about five or six years ago and once I start doing something like that then it becomes a habit. The idea of the doll isn't to bring luck, though, it's to ward off evil spirits.'

The voodoo doll on the rear of the 2005–6 five-time TT winning Shoei.

'This helmet was originally worn a couple of times in practice in 2005 on the AIM Yamaha but I never liked it and then changed it because I felt it was too far away from the original. Any time I came away from the original design it felt like I had no knickers on.'

This is the helmet that John wore to win the Superbike TT in 2009. He was also leading the Senior TT when the chain broke in Ramsey. 'I had set the current outright lap record (131.578mph) before the chain snapped and the helmet has never been worn since I took it off that day.' There are also a lot more commercial logos on this helmet as greater television coverage of the event, including the use of a helmet camera, has increased the opportunities to raise sponsorship.

2005 was the first year with Shoei and this particular helmet was worn in both '05 and '06 to win five TTs – a double on the Yamahas in '05 and a treble on Hondas the following year.

The Superbike and Senior TT winning Shoei helmet from 2011.

The helmet John wore in 2012 on the Shinden electric bike in the TT Zero race. The helmet was only used for one lap of practice and one racing lap.

The Shoei helmet that John wore when winning the Superbike and Superstock TTs in 2012. The red, white and blue colours were incorporated as part of a celebration of the 2012 London Olympics.

2006 BACK WITH THE BIG 'H'

Honda has always been the premier manufacturer racing at the Isle of Man TT and given John's success in 2004 and 2005 they could no longer ignore his talents. For 2006 they made an offer that he could not refuse and he returned to the squad after a two-year absence. The move brought greater security – and immediate success.

'There's no doubt that my race set-up was more planned and organised when I returned to Honda in 2006. I knew exactly what I was getting, and where we were testing and racing. There was nothing wrong with the Yamahas but the Hondas were a good reliable package. I had great mechanics, we were going testing in Spain pre-season and the Dunlop tyres were working well.

'The Honda contract involved a full season of Superstock racing in the British championship and the roads deal included the North West 200 as well as the TT and Ulster Grand Prix. With all the testing and racing I felt strong on the bikes by the time I got to the North West. I had Eugene Laverty's British championship 600, my own Superstock bike that I was riding week in, week out and a purpose-built superbike for the roads that included a lot of the simple things that we had developed over the years at the TT. Low and wide footpegs and wide handlebars might not seem much of a development but all these little modifications made the job good and I wasn't riding somebody else's BSB bike – it was my bike, specially built for me.

'Most important of all, I knew exactly where I stood. There was a testing programme, a racing programme, a wages programme, a bonus structure and I felt part of a bigger effort. There was a budget to make things happen. It felt how it should. Yes, it was more corporate – there were more dealer days, more charity things, more functions but I don't

John wheels his HM Plant Honda Fireblade on to the
Mountain Mile during evening practice in 2006.

mind doing stuff like that. I was employed to do a job, which was to win TTs, and I won three in '06.

'Racing on the short circuits every weekend kept me sharp and the bar was raised again at the TT because I went from 127mph laps to 128s and 129s. The tools I had for the job allowed me to go one step further and although these magical lap times don't really blow my skirt up, it was still cool to follow on from DJ's first 125, 126, and 127mph laps.

'There were only four TT races in '06 – just one 600 race, the Superstock and the two big bike races. The superbike races went to plan – I dropped the clutch, got a good start, concentrated hard for the six laps, had two good pit stops, all pretty straightforward really. The Honda crew is the most consistent on the pit stops. I've had the same guy changing my back wheel for years now. We think about it a lot and we practice and practice the routine.

'I struggled with the 600 at the North West and in TT practice and I had a bit of a diva strop about the set-up. The bike was a missile, definitely the fastest 600 on the track, but it wasn't working for me at the TT. Honda brought a mechanic over from GB and made some changes to the throttle bodies and gearing that altered the characteristics of the engine. In the end, all the moaning I did about the bike paid off – I broke the lap record and won the 600 race. That was really satisfying.

'By the time I went back to Honda in 2006 the TT was definitely the priority for me and my sponsors. That shift in focus, with the TT becoming the centre of my year, came after 2005 when I had a go in the British Superbike championship and, to be brutally honest, I wasn't fast enough. I wanted to go in a different direction after that and Honda wanted me to race in the British Superstock class on the short circuits – they still believed that I could win the title. Doing a short circuit championship like that has kept me on top of my game for the roads and it has remained part of my programme of racing ever since. I'm still doing a full season of competition against top quality riders, pushing hard every weekend.'

John lifts his head slightly above the screen at Mountain Box during practice on the 600cc Honda. Initially he struggled with this bike. 'The engine was set up to give it lots of drive from low down but not so much top speed and I just couldn't get on with it at the TT. We made changes and after all my moaning I won the race and set a new lap record at 123.975mph.'

A couple of spectators watch as John dodges the stone walls and barbed wire at Guthrie's Memorial on his Supersport Honda during evening practice in 2006. 'I never, ever drive around the course. When you are going that slow in a car you can see too clearly all the things that you could hit if you crashed. At racing speed they are just a blur.'

Pulling on his boots in the motorhome moments before the race begins.

Cutting a lonely figure, John climbs the Mountain towards Guthrie's Memorial on the Honda Fireblade superbike during evening practice.

WHEN THE CHEQUERED FLAG FALLS...

Raising both arms in triumph, John takes the chequered flag to win the Senior TT, his third win of the week and his eleventh win in total. It was also his second treble in a single year.

'Give it a rest you pair!' The expression on their son Ewan's face tells its own story as his parents share a celebratory kiss after John's Senior TT win.

Treble number two!

John comes off worst in this ice cream fight with great friends Bruce Anstey and Cameron Donald in the Senior TT winners' enclosure.

It was the third time that John had come first in a week so he deserved a pint in the Senior TT post-race press conference.

A huge crowd welcomes John on the return road after his victory in the Superbike TT in 2006.

2007 130MPH

As the grand old event celebrated its first hundred years John felt he needed to produce something special for the big birthday. The 100mph lap speed barrier had been broken on the fiftieth anniversary and only a new landmark speed would be a fitting milestone. Everyone was looking at the main man to produce and the main man would not disappoint.

'I really wanted to win the big bike races at the Centenary TT and I felt under a lot of pressure to be the first person to do a 130mph lap. Everybody wanted it to happen and I wanted to be the one to do it, to set that milestone.

'There was definitely more pressure all round in 2007 because there were lots more media and people on the Island and there was a lot of expectation that it should be a year when something special happened. I tried to hit the 130 in practice but I didn't because I was trying too hard.

'Conditions were mostly good throughout practice and into race week, although the track was a bit patchy for the opening Superbike race. That kept speeds down to around 128mph. I finished ahead of Guy Martin and Ian Hutchinson to make it an all-Honda podium.

'I rode hard in the Supersport and Superstock races and finished second in both but my focus was on the Senior and on trying to get that 130mph lap. Come race day, conditions were perfect – the roads were dry and plenty of rubber had been laid down on the track over the fortnight to create the kind of grip I wanted. The HM Plant Hondas were mega and I'd only had to make a few small alterations from the year before. Hutchy and I had been on the podium for every race so far that week and I had really enjoyed the Centenary TT.

'I got my head down right from the start of the race and tried to break away. I knew that my second lap was strong and coming into the pits at the end of it I had a special feeling that I had never had before. The crowd was cheering in the grandstand and people were going nuts at Quarterbridge and at Braddan as I started the third lap. I could even hear the shouts and cheers and I'd never heard that before. It wasn't until I got to Ballacraine on that lap and I saw my friend Ian MacIntosh holding my pit board with 130 on it that I realised I had broken the record. The actual speed was 130.354mph.

The 130 road sign had been specially made in anticipation of the landmark speed being achieved, another indication that everyone expected John to break the barrier. He was given the road sign on the Senior podium and his satisfaction is obvious. 'What made that first 130mph lap really special was that it was only done once, on one lap, by one rider. If four or five people had been doing it throughout the race it would have devalued it for me.'

'I took it steady and tried to control the race from the front after that, building a thirty-second cushion over Guy Martin and Hutchy.

'Later that evening Ian sent me a text that simply said 'Bob Mac 1957, John Mac 2007'. I thought that was really cool. [Bob McIntyre was the first rider to lap the Mountain course at over 100mph in 1957.]

'I always say that I would find it hard to choose my favourite TT. The first win in 1999 was special, my first treble in 2004 was great, but 2007 stands out as a really enjoyable year. I started every lap and I finished every lap. There were no frights because I was riding bikes with the best of everything on them and it was the first and only 130mph lap. Plus I got a couple of decent results as well.'

Getting into the spirit of the Centenary TT celebrations, John tries out a vintage Rudge machine during the re-enactment of the original 1907 start at St John's. A field of 100 riders took part in a special lap around the original TT course and John waved them over the finish line with the chequered flag.

John gets blasted with the champagne by runner-up Guy Martin and third-placed Ian Hutchinson on the Superbike TT podium.

John shakes hands with Guy Martin in the winners' enclosure after the Senior TT as, in the background, veteran commentator Murray Walker looks on. 'I get on well with Guy. He's quirky, different, off the wall. He has something to say all the time and he's contagious, infectious. I think he's fantastic for the sport. He was younger then and he thought he was Jack the Lad – he reminded me of myself at that age. But he ruffled me up a little bit at the North West just before the TT, gobbing off about factory riders polishing their motorhomes. I never said a word but it was a fire burning in my belly, I was going to beat him and I did. And that's what I was saying to him here – "I'm off now to polish my motorhome." Guy knew what I meant. There was no malice in it – I just wanted to make the point. Murray Walker was in tears that day – he told me he never thought he would see a 130mph lap in his lifetime.'

Only the front wheel is on the ground as John flicks the HM Plant Honda through Union Mills on his way to his first victory of the Centenary TT in the Superbike race.

John is swamped by a frenzy of photographers
at the end of the Senior TT.

'There is a great sense of relief at this
point. The week is over, I've finished,
I'm home and I'm safe.'

Taking a break during the press launch in 2007,
John looks down the mountain towards Ramsey.

*'I never get to see this, what's behind me.
I am so focused on the track in front that I
don't even realise that all this exists.'*

The spectators at the Raven pub in Ballaugh have a bird's eye view of John as he steers the HM Plant Honda through the village on his way to the first 130mph lap of the Mountain course and victory in the Senior TT.

2008 DOWN TO THE WIRE

Although a cursory glance at the TT record books appears to show a seamless run of success for the Morecambe Missile, there have always been shifts in John's TT career. 2008 was to bring another new association. It also brought a new and very determined rival from south of the equator. As the competition heated up, the margin between success and failure was smaller than at any time in TT history.

'There was a bit of a shift sideways with Honda in '08 because of some kind of politics with the TT that I didn't understand and I ended up riding in Padgett's colours. Only the Superstock bike was supplied from Honda and they ran it in HM Plant colours.

'Results speak for themselves and the Padgett's team had plenty of success at the TT. I knew that Clive Padgett and his boys could build bikes capable of winning. I suppose the only thing that worried me and Clive was that if we didn't win people would say it was because we weren't on HM Plant bikes which people regarded as 'factory'.

'The Fireblade was a new model for '08 and it had been completely revamped with more power from the engine, a different swingarm, an altered riding position, and new wheels and frame. It was a totally different bike and we were going into it blind. Right from the start of practice the bike was a handful, lap times were down and we were really struggling. There was also an issue with the crank sensor and both Guy Martin and I broke down in the Superbike race because of it. Mine quit on lap two at the Bungalow and Guy's Hydrex bike broke down just when it looked like he was going to get his first win.

'I never get bitter when something breaks on the bike. Yes, I have a little moment to myself and then I get over it because I always think that somebody, somewhere, is having a much worse day than me.

'The person who gets more upset about breakdowns than anyone else is Clive. I broke down in the second 600 race that year as well and Clive just disappeared – I thought we were going to find him in the Irish Sea he was so distraught.

'We were back to five races in '08 and I finished second in the first Supersport race and runner-up again in the Superstock race – that elusive Superstock win still hadn't

John on the Padgett's Honda at Creg-Ny-Baa during the Senior TT in 2008. 'The Creg might be the most famous place on the course with the iconic view of Kate's cottage in the background but it's a crap corner. It's just a case of getting it stopped, getting it round and getting out of there. There's nothing to be gained but it does always feel like there's not far to go until the end.'

come. It didn't seem fair to have such bad luck after all the hard work and money that had been spent on the Padgett's TT effort but it definitely meant that there was huge relief when we won the Senior.

'That race was one of the hardest battles I've ever had at the TT, absolutely nip and tuck, wheel to wheel all the way with Cameron Donald. It's the first time that I've been in a race at the TT where I've seen +0.3, +0.8 or -0.6 on my pit boards. It had always been in seconds before, never in tenths of seconds. It is ridiculous on a track like that to have such small gaps between us and the lead swapped nine or ten times during the race before something went wrong with Cameron's bike and I was off the hook a little bit.

'It would have been a grandstand finish if Cameron hadn't hit the problem. He had already had a couple of wins that week and he was riding the best he probably ever had but I had a bit of luck. That's the TT for you and you take the luck when you get it.

'So we managed to keep up the record of winning something every year since 2003 and to see Clive's face at the end was just brilliant.'

John takes the plaudits of the fans along the return road after winning the Senior TT in 2008. 'There is no feeling like coming up that road after winning the Senior TT – 1) it's a relief that it's over and you've won, 2) you're in one piece, 3) you've done a fantastic job, 4) you've made some pennies, 5) you've got some silverware, 6) you're going home and 7) you've probably ensured you've got a job for the next year. What will be strange though will be coming up that slip road after the Senior and not turning into the winners' enclosure because every time I've come up there since 2004, I've been coming up as the winner.'

'That's my mum Christine on the left of this picture in the brown coat, quietly watching me celebrate. She has never missed one of my TT races and she has always been there to see me leave the start line and to cross it again at the end of the race.'

John leaps Ballaugh Bridge on the Padgett's Honda during practice in 2008. 'You approach Ballaugh absolutely flat out in sixth gear at about 180mph and then you go right down into first for the bridge. I always give the throttle a little blip over the top to try to get the front wheel up. I know I'm one of the biggest jumpers over it but it doesn't feel like it on the bike and I don't set out to do it. I still don't jump as high as Finnegan [the late Martin Finnegan] did though.'

John on the Padgett's Honda at Creg-Ny-Baa during the Senior TT in 2008.

John celebrates winning the Senior TT with thousands of fans during the presentation at the grandstand in 2008. 'Everybody had waited for the presentation, they were buying up the T-shirts for their family. I was shocked to see so many people there when I walked out to collect the trophy. I still have my leathers on because I had had a few beers after the race. When I had watched Hizzy, Foggy or Joey getting their trophies I thought it was the coolest thing I'd ever seen if they were still wearing their leathers.'

2009 THE WEAKEST LINK

2009 will always be remembered as the year that MotoGP racing legend Valentino Rossi visited the TT. The hullaballoo around the Italian's arrival overshadowed much of what was going on on the race track but for John there was a new threat to his TT supremacy – and it was coming from within his own team.

'The TT really seemed to be gathering momentum in 2009. There were more big sponsors involved, Valentino Rossi arrived on the Island and there was lots more media attention. For me, it was business as usual. I was back in the HM Plant colours for the TT even though I was riding for Padgett's in the British Superstock championship. I still rode Clive's Superstock bike on the Island.

'There was a lot of talk about Guy Martin in 2009. He's a really popular figure and he was still trying to chase down his first TT win. But I had another man nipping at my heels, my new team-mate Steve Plater.

'I can never rest on my laurels at the TT because there are always new guys coming to the front. It's a good thing because it keeps me on my toes. When somebody like Plater comes along you have to take it really seriously. He is the ultimate professional – he's fast, he's mega-fit, he's focused, he's done his homework and that year he was on the same bike as me. He had been dominant at the North West 200 and had won his first TT the year before. The only thing I could do was beat him on the stopwatch, and knowing that made me sharpen myself up for '09.

'That year I was as fit and strong as I'd ever been and I was scoring regular podiums in the British championship. People say I don't train. I do train – but on my bike, not in the gym. I am always active, always on my bikes, getting bike-fit, whether it's motocrossing, BSB, enduro bikes, mini bikes or testing. I do a lot more riding than most other TT racers.

'But I don't like the gym, it makes me unhappy, puts pressure on me. Sometimes I wish I could do it, maybe lose a bit of weight. But the way I see it, if you're happy messing around on the motocross and enduro bikes, spending a bit of time with your kids and cruising along in life then you ride fast. But if you are pressurising yourself about having to go to the gym, what food to eat, what weight you should be, it beats you down.

Moto GP world champion Valentino Rossi presents John with the winner's trophy after the Superbike TT. 'I had raced against Valentino in the British Grand Prix at Donington in 2000 as a wildcard and he remembered that. He's a multiple world champion and all that but the special thing about him is his knowledge of racing. There was so much going on that day but Valentino told me to come and visit him at the British Grand Prix later in the year and when I did he grilled the ears off me about the TT!'

ISLE OF MAN
ISLE OF MAN
ISLE OF MA
HONDA
HONDA
HONDA
YAMAHA
YAMAHA
VR|46

John and Steve Plater at the 33rd Milestone on the HM Plant Hondas. 'Steve was leading the British Supersport championship and he had won his first TT the year before so I knew that he would be chasing me down.'

2009 race week started great and I won the first Superbike race with Valentino Rossi watching from Bray Hill and the pits. But the week never really happened for me after that. I didn't ride well in the 600 races and I was leading the Superstock race when I hit a rear tyre problem and slipped back to fifth.

'All the disappointment meant that I was well up for the Senior on Friday. Steve had given me a run for my money in the Superbike race and I knew he would be even stronger in the Senior because he was lapping the course at over 130mph now. I really put my heart and soul into the race from the start to try to get a gap. I pushed so hard that the outright lap record went on the second lap. It felt fast but not out of control. I was braking late, getting on the power early, and I had the grip and stability I needed. I was slowing down for the pit stop at the end of the lap.

'But Steve Plater was such a tough competitor and I knew I was never really off the hook with him in the race. I was still pushing hard on lap four because I was being pushed. If I hadn't been so concerned about Steve, if I'd had a comfortable lead, then maybe I wouldn't have changed gear so hard from first to second going out of Parliament Square. And then maybe the chain wouldn't have snapped.

'You can beat yourself up about it and point the finger but at the end of the day the chain broke and I was out of the race.

'People say nobody really knows how fast I could go at the TT because I've never been pushed hard enough on a big bike. That day I was pushed and I set the fastest ever lap – but I didn't win the race.'

TLC – John gives his HM Plant Honda a hug before the start of the opening night of practice.

The TT's fastest bike – HM Plant Honda Fireblade, 2009.

John enjoys the evening sunlight at Rhencullen during practice week but in
the second Supersport race he had one of his biggest scares at this spot.
'The second race was damp and I nearly crashed at Rhencullen. I thought
"I'm dead." It's one of the few times I've felt that at the TT, but I ended up back
on my wheels more through luck than skill and carried on to finish 11th.'

John celebrates winning the Superbike TT with Valentino Rossi and Giacomo Agostini. 'It was very special to be greeted by Rossi and Agostini after winning that TT. They are the two greatest short circuit riders of all time and Ago's a ten-times TT winner. It doesn't get any better than that.'

Valentino Rossi looks on as John leaves the pits after his refuelling stop in the Superbike TT.

'I can never rest on my laurels at the TT but that's a good thing because it keeps me on my toes. There are always new people coming along, pushing to the front. Some of them gob off about what they are going to do and that gives me a bit of drive as well.'

John chats with rivals Michael Dunlop, Cameron Donald and Michael Rutter at the 33rd Milestone.

'Petrol's going up and lap speeds are going up!' On his way to setting the fastest ever lap of the TT Mountain course, John has no time for a comfort stop on his HM Plant Honda in Union Mills.

A disconsolate John with the lap speed plaque from the ancient TT scoreboard that lines Glencrutchery Road. It was his only 'trophy' from the Senior TT after his HM Plant Honda snapped its chain on the fourth lap of the race. The new outright lap record speed of 131.578mph still stands today.

2010 THE SPELL IS BROKEN

The first decade of the new century ended with one man's complete domination of the TT and it wasn't John McGuinness. Not only did his team-mate Ian Hutchinson win every solo race (bar the electric bike race) but John failed to score a podium finish for the first time since 1997. It was a result that would shake his self-belief to its very core.

'I won at the North West 200 in May and I came to the TT feeling really strong so I don't really understand what went wrong in 2010.

'I had the same set-up with the bikes as the previous year and practice had gone well. In the first race I was giving it everything as usual. Then I ran off the road at the end of the Cronk-y-Voddy straight at 180mph. I had grass in my boots where I ran down the bank. Looking back that seemed to symbolise the beginning of the end for me at the 2010 TT, the start of a disastrous week. I survived that scare but I only got as far as Sulby bridge and the bike stopped again with a broken crank sensor.

'I finished seventh and fifth in the two Supersport races, which was pretty average, and in the Superstock I was fourth. I hadn't made the podium in any race and once again it was all down to the Senior. It was a very eventful race for everyone.

'After the first pit stop I was running at the front with Conor, Hutchy and Guy and then the race was red flagged. I was in my rhythm so I was really disappointed that it was stopped until I heard that Guy had crashed at Glen Vine. I immediately thought if he has crashed there he is dead – it's just such a fast corner, 150–160mph. But then reports started to come through that he was sitting up and talking. It was a massive relief.

'So it was back to the pits and a restart over four laps in the afternoon. Again it was nip and tuck between Conor, Hutchy and me. 0.3 of a second is less than the length of a motorbike and that's how close we were. Then, coming out of the Black Dub on the second lap, the wire on my kill switch broke and the bike cut out. I pulled up and kicked the wall. I was absolutely gutted as I watched Conor and Hutchy ride past.

'I ran down to Glen Helen and someone handed me a pint of beer but I was still fuming that I had been forced out of the last three TT Superbike races by poxy little failures that were out of my hands. Then the news came through that Conor had crashed at The Verandah. Suddenly everything changed – Guy and Conor were hurt

A man with a lot on his mind after TT 2010. 'Things were going wrong and I was thinking maybe someone was telling me it was time to stop.'

and in hospital and I was sitting in the sun, still in one piece, with a beer in my hand. It put it all into perspective.

'Things were going great for Hutchy though. He won the Senior to clinch all five TTs, the full gentleman's set. It was the first time anyone had won them all, a massive milestone that has gone down in TT history. I was pleased for him and for Padgett's because it couldn't have gone to a better bloke or a better team. We were team-mates and I had helped Ian earlier in his career so there was some satisfaction in his success.

'But yes, there was envy. I wish I had done it.

'My head had dropped by the time I came away from the Island in 2010 and I thought it's over for me. It was the first year since 1997 that I hadn't made the podium at the TT and it felt like something or someone was telling me I was finished. Things were going wrong and I was thinking maybe it was time to stop.'

John on the Padgett's Honda on the start line of the opening Supersport race in 2010. 'The starter has his hand on my shoulder, waiting for the flag to drop. He could be the last person to touch me but I sometimes wind him up by letting the clutch out a little bit and he pulls me back as the bike starts to creep forward! But at this point all your nerves are gone and there's no messing. I'm just concentrating on the guy with the flag. Once he moves one millimetre I'm off.'

John pulls in for a pit stop during the Supersport race. 'I always try to stay calm in the pits. For the time I am in there I hand the job over to them and let them get on with it. It isn't going to help if I start shouting and screaming. Everybody is doing their best and I never interfere. There's a visor change, a wheel change, I take on a drink, they wipe the screen and the boys fill it up with fuel. Julian, who changes my back wheel, is so cool and collected. Once he has swapped the wheel he lifts the bike off the stand really gently and reaches forward to put the bike into gear and pump up the back brake up – all in one fluid motion.'

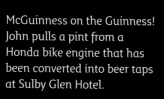

John shoots a game of pool with Stuart Easton in Joey Dunlop's bar in Ballymoney.

McGuinness on the Guinness! John pulls a pint from a Honda bike engine that has been converted into beer taps at Sulby Glen Hotel.

Chatting with his Padgett's Honda teammate Ian Hutchinson before the start of the opening night of TT practice in 2010. Hutchy would make TT history by winning all five races and John's remarkable record of having made the the podium at every TT since 1997 would come to an end.

John shares a joke with the complete line up of 2009 TT winners at the 2010 race launch in Douglas. (L-R) Michael Dunlop (2nd Supersport), Ian Hutchinson (Superstock and 1st Supersport), Steve Plater (Senior), Dave Molyneux (both Sidecar races), John and Rob Barber (TTXGP).

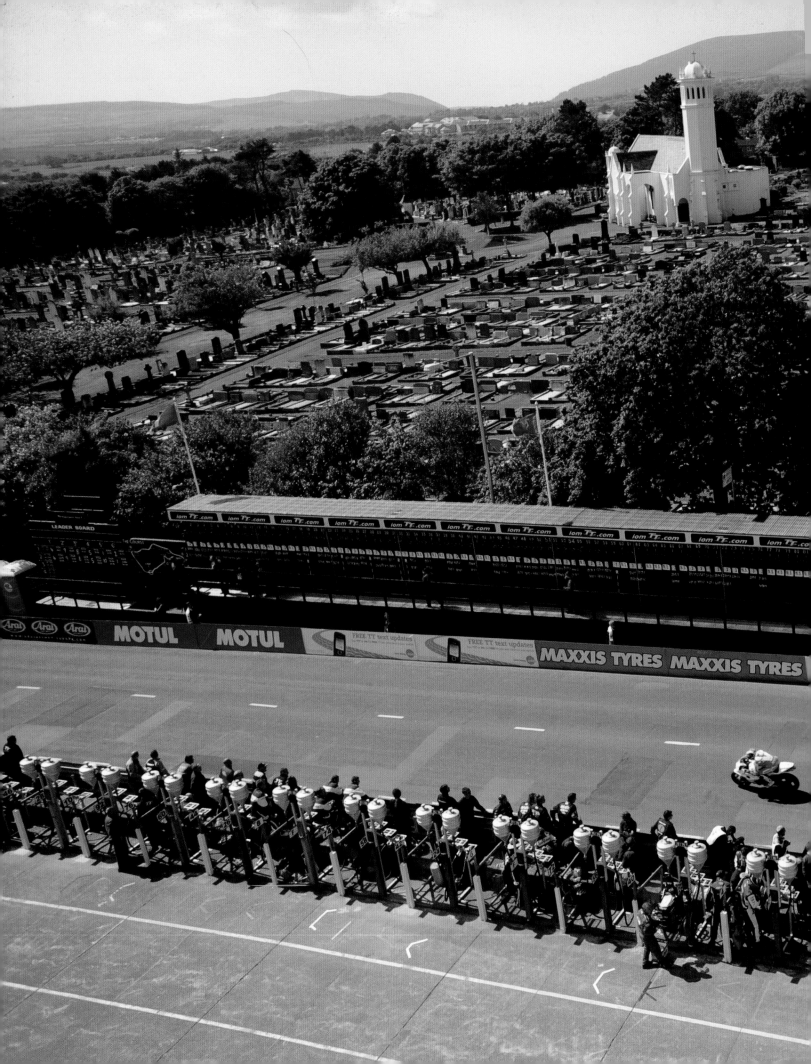

'I never think about the graveyard being there, it never comes into my head. I don't like it, I don't want to be in there any time soon.'

John leaps the Padgett's Honda
Superstock bike over Ballaugh Bridge
during an evening practice session.

John is lost in a moment of reverie as he stands on the Glencrutchery Road start line in 2010. 'I always like to find a little bit of time on my own to mull things over. This is the most famous piece of tarmac in motorsport and I always think about what my heroes have done here, all they achieved. And all that has been lost as well. They have to change those Portakabins though – they look shite.'

MORECAMBE MAN

John McGuinness travels all over the world riding motorbikes, from testing tyres in Malaysia and electric bikes in Japan to racing in locations as far apart as Coleraine and Qatar. Global travel is now part of his job as a professional motorcycle racer but no matter which direction it takes him in, the road back always leads to the same place, his home town of Morecambe. John still lives in the seaside town in which he was born, close to all of his and his wife Becky's family.

'It was a good place to grow up in and now it's a good place for me to raise my kids,' John says proudly.

John would be the first to admit that money was far from plentiful during his childhood but he was always at the centre of the kind of loving family that he tries to provide for his own children today.

'I was watched over by my Granny McGuinness as a nipper.' John recalls. 'She was a great old lady and I stayed with her a lot. She smoked Senior Services nonstop but she kept me safe.'

When his schooldays ended the TT legend-to-be started to serve his time as an apprentice bricklayer and any guided tour of the streets of Morecambe with John includes being shown a variety of buildings that he worked on. They are all still standing.

Once his interest in motorcycles had grown into a desire to compete, the seventeen-year-old turned his hand to one of the town's traditional occupations to help raise the funds to buy his first race bike. Becky's father gathered cockles and mussels at low tide on the huge expanse of sand on Morecambe Bay and he soon had John in tow. 'I bought my first proper race bike, a 1992 TZ250 Yamaha, from the money I made out of collecting mussels,' John fondly remembers.

There were only fifteen TT winners' trophies in the cabinet when this picture was taken – there are nineteen now. And counting.

Two famous Morecambe men together. John with the statue of Eric Morecambe on the promenade of their Lancashire hometown.

John collects mussels on Morecambe Bay. He launched his racing career on the bike he bought with the proceeds of mussel and cockle picking. 'I had to work hard to raise the funds to go racing or it was never going to happen but I could always see myself as a TT winner at the end of the dark tunnel. Nothing else made any sense to me.'

Although it can be a long haul from the far north west to some of the racetracks further south, the roads of the Isle of Man are much closer by. The ferry to Mona's Isle departs every day from the port of Heysham, just a couple of miles from the door of the McGuinness family home.

'The TT is really my local race, as the crow flies,' John says, laughing. 'But when my dad was racing he still missed the ferry to the Island the first time that he entered the TT!'

John has been a regular visitor to the Island since his early days as a stowaway on his BMX. His achievements have not gone unrecognised in his home county either and in 2007 John was granted the Freedom of the City of Lancaster by his local council, the first sportsman ever to be made an Honorary Freeman in the borough.

'I am really proud of that award, both as a Morecambe man and as a bike racer,' John says, smiling. 'Apparently it allows me to drive sheep up and down the promenade a couple of times a year as well.'

John and his daughter Maisie Grace wash the car together. 'John has a pre-TT ritual,' his wife Becky explains. 'He cuts the grass, cleans the house, cleans the cars, cleans the garage, hoovers everything. There is a kind of obsession about it, and a fear. He sometimes tells people that he never buys a return ticket for the ferry just in case something goes wrong, but I think that's just because he's so lazy and disorganised!'

Childhood sweethearts and partners for twenty-three years, John and Becky were married in their home town in April 2012. As Becky put the finishing touches to her make up in the hall mirror she needed no reminding of what her husband-to-be does for a living. John's replica centenary Senior TT winning HM Plant Fireblade, a gift from Honda in recognition of his achievement in setting the first ever 130mph lap of the Mountain Course, takes centre stage in the entrance to their Morecambe home.

2011 NORMAL SERVICE IS RESUMED

A major new racing initiative from Honda for 2011 indicated that the Japanese factory had perhaps more faith in their star TT rider than he had in himself at that time. Not only would John be part of the new world endurance squad, but to all intents and purposes the team was named in his honour as well. With Ian Hutchinson, the golden boy of TT 2010, sidelined by injury the new team provided just the boost that John needed to get back on to the top step of the podium.

'Everything changed in 2011. Honda rang up and said they wanted to talk. I thought it was going to be about getting my P45 but instead they said they wanted to go world endurance racing. It is one of the best things that has ever happened to me because I get lots of testing and racing, plenty of time on the bike. Doing a twenty-four-hour race stretches you physically and mentally – a six-lap TT seems a lot easier afterwards.

'I was still involved with Clive on the Supersport and Superstock bikes and I chose to start at number 1 again. I hadn't been ready for it in 1999 but I'd been around the game long enough by 2011 to handle it. There'd just be me, the stopwatch and the track so no room for excuses.

'For the TT the team was the same as the Honda team had been in previous years – same infrastructure, same people. We weren't trying to fix something that wasn't broken. The name was changed to Honda TT Legends and we had a new colour scheme. I liked the iconic colours and the name opened everybody's eyes – everywhere I go people talk to me about the TT now. Maybe there was a bit more pressure, even a bit of embarrassment, about being called a 'TT Legend' but as long as the bikes kept going I didn't mind.

'And in 2011 the bikes kept going.

'At the end of 2010 I wasn't in a great place but I came back and won in 2011. Even though things hadn't gone well the year before, I had tried to take away the positives: I hadn't forgotten how to ride the TT and I'd been lapping at 131mph in the Senior

Joy – and relief – as John celebrates his Superbike TT victory in 2011.

before the bike quit. Yes, it was easier in 2011 because Hutchy and Conor had been sidelined by injures from their 2010 crashes but it was never going to be a cake-walk. Bruce Anstey showed us that when he did a 131.4mph lap in practice and made us all look average.

'I got stuck in straight away in the Superbike race and I followed my tried and tested TT race plan of going for a fast start, driving on to open a gap and then consolidating that lead with a good pit stop. After that I was able to control the race from the front by watching my pit boards. I have one at Ballacraine, one at Gwen's and another one coming out of the Bungalow. MacIntosh is always at Ballacraine. The boards keep me constantly informed. I can see straight away whether I need to push on or if I can nurse the bike a little bit. I followed exactly the same strategy in the Senior and it paid off both times.

'Although I didn't win either of the Supersport races or the Superstock I was competitive. I did my fastest ever lap on a 600 – 126.226mph – in the first race and finished fifth and I was second in the B race. I pushed really hard on the Stocker but Michael Dunlop pushed even harder and I was second yet again.

'I had been waiting to get back into my groove at the TT since the moment that chain broke in the Senior in 2009. Nothing came in 2010, the bikes let me down, and I had to wait a bit longer. But it was worth the wait. A win is always worth the wait.'

The lady of the house and her dog have a grandstand view of John as he wheelies the TT Legends Honda past the cottage at Rhencullen during TT practice in 2011.

2007 was the centenary of the TT races but as the race had been moved from the old St John's course to the Mountain circuit in 1911, 2011 was the hundreth anniversary of racing on the Mountain course. On an early spring morning the TT's top stars – Keith Amor, Ian Hutchinson, Guy Martin and Conor Cummins – joined John in the shadow of Snaefell for this photograph.

John and his team-
mate Keith Amor line
up on the TT Legends
Hondas at the start of
the opening practice
session for the 2011 TT.

Steering the Padgett's
Superstock Honda
down the narrow main
street in Kirkmichael
village during evening
practice in 2011.

John lines up beside Michael
Dunlop at the start of the
Senior TT practice lap.

'This was funny because Michael tried to hold back so
that he could follow me and I was holding back so that
he wouldn't be able to – I didn't want to give anything
away. So neither of us was going anywhere!'

John goes past the front door of Quayle's grocery shop in Kirkmichael village at 170mph on the TT Legends Honda during practice in 2011.

John gets a congratulatory hug from Guy Martin after he had beaten the Suzuki rider in the Senior TT. 'Guy told me I was his hero.'

'I had been waiting for this moment since 2009. A win is always worth the wait.'

All eyes are on the winner on the Superbike podium as John displays his relief at being back on the top step after a year's absence.

2012 ADDING TO THE TALLY

With the Senior TT called off for the first time in 105 years, John lost the opportunity to race for his traditional Superbike double in 2012. But he still scored a brace of wins by taking the one race that had always evaded him. Moving closer to twenty victories also brought inevitable speculation about whether he could become the most successful TT racer of all time.

'Apart from having a couple of fake headlight stickers on the front, it was the same TT Legends Honda, the same colours and the same team for 2012. I did have a plan to try to make the bike better in '12 and we changed the wheelbase, we tried traction control and anti-wheelie, altered the suspension link and loads of other things but nothing really worked so we went back to all of the original settings.

'Our Honda might not be the fastest out there or have the latest technology – the bike is a 2008 model and the forks are the same as they were in 2007 – but it is a tried and tested package that I have confidence in. There are no electronic aids. It's the connection from your brain to your wrist to your arse to the back tyre that makes it all work.

'I got a really inspirational text the night before the Superbike race from Formula One driver Mark Webber. We became friends after he visited the TT with his dad in 2008. The TT just blew Mark away – he said it was the most amazing thing he'd ever seen in motorsport.

'His text said: Cool head champ, it's all about you. Focus fully on your own performance and the result will take care of itself. You are riding mega at the moment, stay in the moment mentally, which you have done thousands of times around there before. Nerves are good, it means that you want it. Enjoy mate, see you tomorrow.

Out of the darkness. With the TT Legends
Honda Fireblade now sporting stick-on
headlights, John exits Greeba Castle during
evening practice for TT 2012.

John steers the Padgett's Honda over Braddan Bridge on his way to winning his first Superstock TT.

What might have been – John takes a last look at the Senior TT trophy before it is packed away. The 2012 Senior TT was cancelled for the first time in the event's 105 year history due to bad weather.

'And Mark was there when I came up the return road after I won the race.

'I knew that Cameron, Guy and Bruce would all be in the mix in that Superbike race. Cameron had been strong in practice and he gave me a bit of a push for a while before he fell back. You never really know what you are going to get from Guy but you always know that old Bruce will give it a go. I knew we could make up some time in the pit stops and we got five seconds in each one and that's a lot of time to make up when you're going at the pace we were. It was a bit windy and misty on the Mountain at one stage and I thought there might be a red flag but we kept going and in the end it was a bit of a textbook race really.

'That doesn't mean it was easy in any way, it never is at the TT. But we were well prepared and had a good strategy that we made work in the race.

'We are all going faster than ever in the races now and the racing is closer than ever. We are only split by

Exiting the Gooseneck on the Shinden electric bike. John is on his way to a 100mph plus lap in the TT Zero race.
Picture by Charles McQuillan

tenths of a second. All the bikes and the tyres are very similar and everybody has access to all of the same kit and technology as well. It evens everything up.

'A few years ago you could hide under the radar a little because it would only be announced on the radio commentary what the time gaps were. You didn't really know where the time was being won or lost and it was hard to compare yourself with anyone else. But with today's transponder timing there is nowhere to hide. Every lap is divided into sectors and each sector time is recorded so everyone knows where they are strong or weak and they can make comparisons. Riders know where they have to up their game.

'Having said that, it's a bit of a mystery why the outright lap record hasn't been broken since 2009. Maybe it's just down to the conditions not being so good. They were perfect in '09 – the racing line was clean and the weather was good.

'I rode in Padgett's colours again in the two Supersport races in 2012 and I finished fourth and fifth in both. And I finally got the Superstock win I wanted. I suppose I had always had a bit of a mental block about that race but I looked down the line at everyone else before the start and thought I can win this – my tyres are hot, the gearings are right, the chassis is fantastic, the bike is good, it's time to win. Hutchy did 130.741mph two years ago on the same bike, which is the best TT lap in history as far as I'm concerned, so I thought, let's stop buggering around here, and I nailed it.

'I really enjoyed riding the Mugen Shinden in the electric bike race. I don't really see it as the future, at least not yet, because the bikes cost a ridiculous amount to build. But I loved every part of the experience of working with the Japanese Mugen team. It reminded me of those old iconic pictures when the Japanese teams first competed at the TT in the fifties and sixties. They were pioneers then and they are again now.

'It made history that the Senior TT was called off in 2012. That had never happened in 105 years but it was the right decision in my opinion because the track was too wet in some parts to race on a superbike. It will never please everyone when you have to make a call like that but that's what the Clerk of the Course had to do.

'I was really disappointed not to have the chance to race for another

John dodges the Manx walls on the Honda TT Legends Fireblade at Guthrie's Memorial during the second TT practice session.

John is congratulated by his friend, Formula One driver Mark Webber, after winning the Superbike TT.

big bike win but the two wins I did get have taken my tally up to nineteen now and people are starting to talk about me beating Joey's record of twenty-six. But I've still got to find seven just to match Joey. I am miles away but it would be the icing on the cake if I could do it and I suppose it's not impossible.

'I'm forty now, stronger than ever, and I'm still winning races. Joey had won fourteen by the time he was my age but age is just a number as he proved when he won three TTs when he was forty-eight in 2000. As long as I've still got my health and the desire to win then I want to carry on.

'So no, there's still no thought of retirement.

'It's not over yet.'

THE STORY SO FAR

- First man to lap at 128mph, 129mph, 130mph and 131mph
- Outright lap record holder since 2004
- More 130mph+ laps than any other rider
- More 125mph+ laps than any other rider
- More 120mph+ laps than any other rider

- 52 Silver replicas, 3 Bronze replicas
- 5 x Winner of Joey Dunlop Trophy (overall TT Championship winner)
- 6 x Winner of Jimmy Simpson Trophy (fastest lap of the meeting)
- 7 x Winner of Norman Brown Trophy (fastest lap of the Senior race)
- 6 x Winner of John Williams Trophy (fastest lap of the Superbike race)

Year	Race	No of laps	Machine	Result	Fastest Lap	Replica	Notes
1996	Lightweight 250cc	4	250cc Paul Bird Honda	15th*	111.49	Bronze	*TT debut
1997	Lightweight 250cc	4	250cc Paul Bird Aprilia	3rd*	116.83	Silver	*Recorded his first TT podium
	Ultra-Lightweight 125cc	4	125cc Paul Bird Aprilia	12th	106.29	Bronze	
	Junior 600cc	4	600cc Clucas Honda	24th*	112.43	n/a	*The only race John's has finished without winning a replica
1998	Lightweight 250cc	2	250cc Vimto Honda	3rd	98.01	Silver	
	Ultra-Lightweight 125cc	4	125cc Vimto Honda	Retired*	103.98	n/a	*Union Mills – broken gearbox, lap 3
	Senior	6	500cc Vimto Honda	Retired*	119.21	n/a	*33rd Milestone – out of fuel, lap 6
1999	Formula One	4	500cc Vimto Honda	Retired*	116.70	n/a	*Pits – broken oil seal, end of lap 2
	Lightweight 250cc	4	250cc Vimto Honda	1st*	118.29	Silver	*First TT win and new class lap record, which can never be beaten
	Senior	6	500cc Vimto Honda	7th	121.15*	Silver	*Recorded his first 120mph+ lap
2000	Formula One	6	1000cc Vimto Honda	3rd*	121.22	Silver	*Recorded his first Superbike podium
	Lightweight 250cc	3	250cc Vimto Honda	Retired*	115.80	n/a	*Quarter Bridge – cracked cylinder head, lap 3
	Singles	4	720cc Chrysalis AMDM	1st	111.43	Silver	
	Senior	6	1000cc Vimto Honda	4th	121.40	Silver	
2002	Formula One	6	954cc Honda	2nd	124.55	Silver	
	Lightweight 400cc	4	400cc Honda	7th	107.70	Silver	
	Production 1000cc	4	954cc Honda	6th	120.94	Silver	
	Junior 600cc	4	600cc Honda	Retired*	119.23	n/a	*11th Milestone – broken conrod, lap 2
	Production 600cc	3	600cc Honda	10th	116.33	Silver	
	Senior	6	954cc Honda	3rd	125.55*	Silver	*Recorded his first 125mph+ lap
2003	Formula One	6	998cc Monstermob Ducati	3rd	125.39	Silver	
	Lightweight 400cc	4	400cc RLR Honda	1st	111.36	Silver	
	Production 1000cc	3	999cc Monstermob Ducati	Retired*	118.69	n/a	*Pits – oil leak, end of lap 2
	Junior 600cc	4	600cc Valmoto Triumph	10th	120.74	Silver	
	Production 600cc	2	600cc Valmoto Triumph	18th	113.87	Bronze	
	Senior	4	998cc Monstermob Ducati	2nd	125.90	Silver	
2004	Formula One	4	1000cc R1 Yamaha	1st*	127.68*	Silver	*First 'big bike' TT win – new outright lap record
	Lightweight 400cc	4	400cc RLR Honda	1st	112.04	Silver	
	Production 1000cc	3	1000cc Yamaha	2nd	125.03	Silver	
	Junior 600cc	4	600cc Yamaha	1st	122.87*	Silver	*New class lap record – completes his first TT hat-trick
	Production 600cc	3	600cc Yamaha	3rd	118.47	Silver	
	Senior	4	1000cc Yamaha	Retired*	127.19	n/a	*Kirk Michael – broken clutch, lap 3

Year	Race	No of laps	Machine	Result	Fastest Lap	Replica	Notes
2005	Superbike	6	1000cc AIM Yamaha	1st	126.88	Silver	
	Superstock 1000cc	3	1000cc AIM Yamaha	Retired*	n/a	n/a	*Bungalow – front wheel puncture, lap 1
	Junior 600cc 'A'	4	600cc AIM Yamaha	2nd	121.79	Silver	
	Junior 600cc 'B'	4	600cc AIM Yamaha	Retired*	n/a	n/a	*Mountain Mile – dropped valve, lap 1
	Senior	6	1000cc AIM Yamaha	1st	127.33	Silver	
2006	Superbike	6	1000cc HM Plant Honda	1st	127.933*	Silver	*New outright lap record (broken in the Senior later in the week)
	Superstock 1000cc	4	1000cc HM Plant Honda	5th	124.558	Silver	
	Supersport 600cc	4	600cc HM Plant Honda	1st	123.975*	Silver	*New lap record
	Senior	6	1000cc HM Plant Honda	1st	129.451*	Silver	*First man to lap at more than 128mph (lap 1) and 129mph (lap 2), new outright lap record, completes second TT hat-trick
2007	Superbike	6	1000cc HM Plant Honda	1st	128.279*	Silver	
	Superstock 1000cc	4	1000cc HM Plant Honda	2nd	127.174	Silver	
	Supersport 600cc	4	600cc Padgetts Honda	2nd	125.096	Silver	
	Senior	6	1000cc HM Plant Honda	1st	130.354*	Silver	*First man to lap at more than 130mph, new outright lap record
2008	Superbike	6	1000cc Padgetts Honda	Retired*	128.617	n/a	*Bungalow – broken crank sensor, lap 2
	Superstock 1000cc	4	1000cc Honda	2nd	127.379	Silver	
	Supersport 600cc 'A'	4	600cc Padgetts Honda	2nd	124.127	Silver	
	Supersport 600cc 'B'	4	600cc Padgetts Honda	Retired*	120.492	n/a	*Pits – end of lap 1, water pump oil seal
	Senior	6	1000cc Padgetts Honda	1st	129.263	Silver	
2009	Superbike	6	1000cc HM Plant Honda	1st	130.442	Silver	
	Supersport 600cc 'A'	4	600cc HM Plant Honda	5th	125.064	Silver	
	Superstock 1000cc	4	1000cc Padgetts Honda	5th	128.538	Silver	
	Supersport 600cc 'B'	4	600cc HM Plant Honda	11th	119.302	Silver	
	Senior	6	1000cc HM Plant Honda	Retired*	131.578mph	n/a	*Parliament Square – broken chain, lap 4. First man to lap at more than 131mph, new outright lap record
2010	Superbike	6	1000cc HM Plant Honda	Retired*	n/a	n/a	*Sulby Bridge – broken crank sensor, lap 1
	Supersport 600cc 'A'	4	600cc Padgetts Honda	7th	124.691	Silver	
	Superstock 1000cc	4	1000cc Padgetts Honda	4th	128.148	Silver	
	Supersport 600cc 'B'	4	600cc Padgetts Honda	5th	125.732	Silver	
	Senior	6	1000cc HM Plant Honda	Retired*	131.410	n/a	*Glen Helen – broken kill switch wire, lap 2
2011	Superbike	6	1000cc Honda TT Legends	1st	131.199	Silver	
	Supersport 600cc 'A'	4	600cc Padgetts Honda	5th	126.226*	Silver	*Personal best lap on 600cc Supersport machine
	Superstock 1000cc	4	1000cc Padgetts Honda	2nd	128.614	Silver	
	Supersport 600cc 'B'	4	600cc Padgetts Honda	2nd	125.629	Silver	
	Senior	6	1000cc Honda TT Legends	1st	131.248	Silver	
2012	Superbike	6	1000cc Honda TT Legends	1st	130.483	Silver	
	Supersport 600cc 'A'	4	600cc Padgetts Honda	4th	125.099	Silver	
	Superstock 1000cc	4	1000cc Padgetts Honda	1st	128.806	Silver	
	TT Zero	1	Shinden Mugen	2nd	102.215	Silver	
	Supersport 600cc 'B'	4	600cc Padgetts Honda	5th	124.883	Silver	

Ewan and Maisie Grace are always at their dad's side, especially when he is collecting the silverware.

First published in 2012 by Blackstaff Press, 4c Heron Wharf,
Sydenham Business Park, Belfast BT3 9LE, Northern Ireland

Text © Stephen Davison, 2012
Photographs © Stephen Davison/Pacemaker Press International,
except where indicated
All rights reserved

Stephen Davison has asserted his right under the Copyright, Designs
and Patents Act 1988 to be identified as the author of this work.

Designed by seagulls.net
Printed by Rotolito Lombarda

A CIP catalogue record for this book is available from the British Library

ISBN 978-0-85640-902-8

www.blackstaffpress.com
www.pacemakerpressintl.com